T0310544

Corporate Foreign Exchange Risk Management

Håkan Jankensgård
Alf Alviniussen
Lars Oxelheim

WILEY

This edition first published 2020

© 2020 John Wiley & Sons Ltd

Registered office

John Wiley & Sons Ltd, The Atrium, Southern Gate, Chichester, West Sussex, PO19 8SQ, United Kingdom

For details of our global editorial offices, for customer services and for information about how to apply for permission to reuse the copyright material in this book please see our website at www.wiley.com.

Library of Congress Cataloging-in-Publication Data

Names: Jankensgård, Håkan, author. | Alviniussen, Alf, author. | Oxelheim, Lars, author.
Title: Corporate foreign exchange risk management / Håkan Jankensgård, Alf Alviniussen, Lars Oxelheim.
Description: Hoboken, New Jersey : John Wiley & Sons, Inc., [2020] | Includes index.
Identifiers: LCCN 2019047749 (print) | LCCN 2019047750 (ebook) | ISBN 9781119598862 (hardback) | ISBN 9781119598916 (adobe pdf) | ISBN 9781119598909 (epub)
Subjects: LCSH: Foreign exchange market. | Corporations—Finance. | Financial risk management.
Classification: LCC HG3851 .O94 2020 (print) | LCC HG3851 (ebook) | DDC 658.15/5—dc23
LC record available at https://lccn.loc.gov/2019047749
LC ebook record available at https://lccn.loc.gov/2019047750

Cover Design: Wiley
Cover Image: © ZGPhotography/Shutterstock

Set in 11.5/14pt, STIXTwoText by SPi Global, Chennai, India.

Printed and bound by CPI Group (UK) Ltd, Croydon, CR0 4YY

10 9 8 7 6 5 4 3 2 1

Contents

Acknowledgements

The authors would like to express their heartfelt thanks to the following individuals for having contributed towards the final product: John Fraser, Hydro One Networks Inc.; Delroy Hunter, University of South Florida; Linus Svensson, KPMG; Fredrik Ericsson, KPMG; Jörgen Carlsson, Lund University.

About the Authors

Håkan Jankensgård obtained his MSc in Finance from Lund University, Sweden, in 2001, after which he took up a position as risk manager at Norsk Hydro ASA, at the time a Norwegian industrial conglomerate. This task involved developing the company's corporate risk management programme and building a risk model to support management's strategic decision-making. Beginning in 2004 he worked as an independent consultant in risk management, specializing in developing decision-support tools that quantify firms' risk-return profile as a function of corporate policies.

Simultaneously with his career as a consultant, Dr Jankensgård pursued a PhD at Lund University, which was completed in 2011. His doctoral thesis is entitled *Essays on Corporate Risk Management* and consists of seven studies on various aspects of risk management in firms. The thesis was awarded the Jan Wallander and Tom Hedelius Stipend, which made it possible to focus exclusively on research for three years. During this time, Dr Jankensgård deepened his research into firms' risk management strategies but also broadened it to cover various other topics in finance, such as the financing

ix

of corporate investment, the effects of information asymmetries, the role of corporate ownership, and volatility in financial markets.

In 2016 Dr Jankensgård became Associate Professor in Corporate Finance at the Department of Business Administration, Lund University. He continues to publish in prestigious academic journals, whilst also teaching Master's-level courses in corporate risk management and valuation. His main research interests are why and how firms use financial derivatives to manage risk, and developing applied frameworks for managing risk that connect the theory of corporate risk management with practice.

Alf Alviniussen graduated from the Norwegian School of Economics and Business Administration, then started work at Norsk Hydro ASA, Oslo, Norway, as an assistant treasurer in 1969. In the following decades the company transformed from mainly a local fertilizer producer to also become a global conglomerate comprising crude and refined oil, aluminium and magnesium, petrochemicals, salmon farming, and so on. About 10–15 years ago the company was gradually split up. Today, aluminium products and hydroelectric power are the primary businesses.

In 1980 Mr Alviniussen was appointed group treasurer, a position he held for more than 20 years. From 1986 his responsibilities also included being president of Hydro Finans, an internal bank for the group. This internal bank carried out a variety of treasury operations and had employees in 12 countries.

As treasurer, Mr Alviniussen was heavily involved in international merger and acquisition projects, as well as greenfield projects. These growth activities put a major strain on treasury, not only from a funding and risk management perspective, but also in the integration of treasury operations, cash management, and relations to banks.

In 2001 Mr Alviniussen took over a position as senior vice president of corporate finance, heading financial planning and risk management, a position he held until retirement in 2011. Thereafter he has acted as a consultant within finance and treasury. From 2013 to 2016 Mr Alviniussen was appointed a member of the Banking Stakeholder Group of the European Banking Authority (EBA), and held a similar position in the European Insurance and Occupational Pensions Authority (EIOPA) in 2016. Both institutions are part of the European System of Financial Supervisors.

Lars Oxelheim is Professor of International Business and Finance at the School of Business and Law, University of Agder, Norway and at Lund University, Sweden. He is affiliated to the Research Institute of Industrial Economics (IFN), an honorary professor at Fudan University, Shanghai, and founding chairman of the Swedish Network for European Studies in Economics and Business (SNEE).

Dr Oxelheim's research interests are in the area of the interplay between the firm and its macroeconomic environment, encompassing economic and financial integration as well as managerial aspects, corporate governance, and risk management. Dr Oxelheim's has authored, co-authored, or edited some 45 research books and is the author of a large number of research articles published in international business, finance, and economic journals. He has been awarded several national and international awards for his research.

Dr Oxelheim's is an active member of several international research networks and serves on the editorial board of a number of journals. He is a delegate of the Royal Swedish Academy of Engineering Sciences (IVA), the Royal Society of Letters at Lund, and elected fellow of the European International Business Academy (EIBA).

Preface

Foreign exchange risk management (FXRM) is one of those topics that one never stops learning new things about. It is so complex and oftentimes counterintuitive that a firm grip on it keeps eluding us – even after a sustained effort over many years. Surprises and 'aha' moments continue to turn up even well after we have begun to think of ourselves as somewhat experienced and knowledgeable in the area. Nor does it take a very large business operation for FX exposures to become so intricate that our common sense and back-of-the-envelope calculations fail to reliably guide us.

Managers intent on managing exposures to FX may, given these limitations of our intuitive assessments, seek guidance in the literature. The available texts on FXRM generally fall into one of two main categories. One is the analysis of the risk management decision in mainstream academic finance. Textbooks in international finance, for example, fall into this category. The cases used have in common that they take place in a stylized setting that abstracts away from various real-world complexities: the exposures are known; there is no uncertainty about any decision parameter; there are no side-effects due to the accounting of the transactions; no distracting self-interest on the part of the decision-makers. Instead, the focus is on laying bare the principles that dictate the correct decision from an economic perspective. The usefulness of this approach lies in the fact that it identifies some core determinants of optimal decision-making under uncertainty. But simplifying away so many of the factors that actually matter is also a limitation; the decision situation is hardly ever served up so neatly in the real world.

The second main category of writing on FXRM are books and online 'guidance papers' on hedge accounting. These works are of a technical nature, dealing with the complicated and arcane accounting rules that surround the use of derivatives. The issue of how to construct and execute hedging positions in light of these standards has, it seems, taken on a life of its own. A broader discussion about the purpose of FXRM and how it relates to overall corporate performance is generally lacking. It is simply taken for granted that the derivative is desirable: it is all about the details.

What prompted us to write this book was the feeling that there was a need for something that finds a balance between analysing the economics of the risk management decision, on the one hand, and a reasonable discussion about the accounting consequences of alternative courses of action, on the other hand. The present book, therefore, aims to take the golden middle path. We have been motivated by a desire to present the economic principles that should guide FXRM, while being mindful of the accounting and organizational realities that face real-world decision-makers.

In particular, it is naïve to think that performance numbers impacted by accounting rules do not matter. The view that 'it is just accounting' is simply not realistic. The reality for most managers is a never-ending attention on numbers that is heavily influenced by these accounting rules. However, letting the accounting considerations determine how we go about FXRM would be placing the cart before the horse.

Instead, the book outlines an integrated perspective that re-examines and challenges the received wisdom about FXRM and its role in the corporation. By 'integrated' we mean measuring and managing the impact of FX on multiple levels of performance, arguing that the ways in which FXRM simultaneously affects cash flow, net income, and the balance sheet must be thoroughly understood. Integrated also refers to the way the firm organizes the FXRM function. Rather than delegating FX policy to the treasury department, as has been the case traditionally, this book envisions managing FX exposures in a board-supervised process for integrated risk management. This entails, among other things, choosing the FX policies that achieve the best risk–return profile for the firm as a whole, considering other risk exposures as well as important performance targets, rather than letting them be determined in a 'silo' context based on a narrow and limited view of corporate performance.

While the book aims to be an actionable guide to decision-making, we draw on the latest academic research in corporate risk management to accomplish this goal. The key insights from several decades of research are presented in a simple and accessible manner. The authors are also able to draw on their own research on risk management. Lars Oxelheim pioneered the study of corporate exposure to macroeconomic risk, including foreign exchange, in the 1980s, and has since regularly published empirical investigations and methodological advances on this topic. Håkan Jankensgård has researched extensively into why and how firms manage risks and, together with Alf Alviniussen, developed risk management frameworks that bridge theory and practice. Alf Alviniussen also brings insights from over 40 years of experience from leading positions in treasury and risk management in Norsk Hydro ASA, then an industrial conglomerate, now a leading integrated aluminium producer.

The book should appeal to any business professional who has some responsibility for, or contact with, performance numbers affected by FX fluctuations. Often, firms struggle to make sense of the various ways in which FX influences the numbers they present. Providing a clear and convincing explanation of the mechanisms behind these effects creates a better understanding of how the firm's performance is actually developing.

The book will also enable professionals to take a more proactive approach to FXRM. The ultimate goal is improved decision-making. We undertake a comprehensive review of the various benefits of FXRM, thus building up the 'business case' for a systematic effort aimed at managing the firm's risk profile. Unlike many texts available on risk management, however, we also present a realistic picture of the costs related to FXRM, allowing for a trade-off between the pros and cons. Ultimately, there should be a convincing case to be made that the benefits are larger and that FXRM leaves the firm's shareholders better off.

The book should also appeal to students of business administration who seek a better understanding of corporate performance and how it is exposed to FX risk. It could be a valuable complement to textbooks in university-level courses on finance or risk management. Our focus has been on developing a narrative aimed at 'connecting the dots', and putting the various parts of FXRM in a broader perspective. These features of the book should enhance the student's understanding of the subject matter compared to textbooks, which by necessity are more fragmented. For the reasons discussed above, it also serves to bridge the two worlds of finance and accounting, which rarely get a unified treatment at universities.

FXRM is an exciting and intellectually stimulating topic. It is also of considerable practical importance. We feel confident in predicting that anyone who studies and masters the principles outlined in this book will quickly become highly appreciated for being able to provide clear answers to the often puzzling FX-related questions that are, at frequent intervals, brought up by various people in the organization. After reading this book, be prepared to become the go-to person.

Key Terms and Abbreviations

Adjusted net monetary position The net monetary position adjusted for items that are unexposed from a net income perspective due to the functional currency being identical to the transaction unit

AL Assets and liabilities

CTGL Currency translation gains and losses (relating to non-monetary assets, to be reported in other comprehensive income)

ERM Enterprise risk management

Foreign currency Any currency other than the home currency

Functional currency The currency in which a legal unit measures and reports its financial performance

FVA Fair value accounting

FX Foreign exchange: the need to convert units of one currency into units of another currency

FXGL   Foreign exchange gains and losses (relating to monetary assets, to be reported in net income)

FXRM   Foreign exchange risk management

GL   Gains and losses

Home currency   The currency in which the corporate group measures and reports financial performance. That is, the functional currency of the parent company

IRM   Integrated risk management

Monetary asset/liability   An asset or liability with a fixed number of units of currency to be received or paid

Net AL position   The sum of all assets denominated in a foreign currency net of the sum of all liabilities denominated in that currency

Net monetary position   The sum of all monetary assets denominated in a foreign currency net of the sum of all monetary liabilities denominated in that currency

OCI   Other comprehensive income

PPE   Property, plant, and equipment (net of accumulated depreciation)

Transaction currency   The currency in which a transaction is executed. It is also the currency in which a monetary AL is denominated. If a company takes up a loan in US dollars, the dollar is the transaction currency

Introduction

An exchange rate is the price of one country's currency in units of another currency. For example, on 12 August 2019, the USD/EUR exchange rate was 0.8927. This is the price of one US dollar expressed in terms of euros. It is the rate any treasurer or accountant dealing with these currencies would use to convert his or her cash flows (or assets) into units of the home currency on that day. They do so because a company operating internationally must be able to express its financial position in home currency terms.

This might give the impression that exchange rates are merely relative prices that are observed in the market and then applied in the everyday administration of a company. Nothing could be further from the truth. The exchange of foreign currencies is big business, and part of the agenda of world leaders and corporate management teams around the globe.

As this book is being written, the USA is embroiled in a rancorous trade war with China. While the grievances of US policymakers with China are many and varied, a key claim backing the hard line taken is that the Chinese government has been heavily manipulating the value of their currency (the renminbi). Such manipulation, the argument goes, keeps the value of the renminbi artificially low vis-à-vis the US dollar, creating an unfair advantage for Chinese exporters in the US market. Obviously, US firms also find it harder to make inroads into the Chinese market when the US dollar is strong. Considering the size of these two consumer markets, the sums at stake are enormous.

Accusations of foul play are not only directed at China. Some European countries have also been reviled for pursuing a kind of trade war against the USA. In this case, the culprit is the low interest rate set by the European Central Bank. This rate was brought historically low after the European debt crisis that erupted in 2009 in an attempt to stimulate growth in the euro-area and to bring back the inflation rate to its target level. The argument here is that the low interest rate weakens the euro, again making it harder for American companies to defend their market shares.

Exchange rates impact the competitiveness of important sectors of the economy, and therefore job creation, and this is why governments care about them. Firms have a more immediate concern in that exchange rates determine the home currency value of their foreign exchange-denominated assets, liabilities, and cash flows in every quarter. Profit margins, market shares, and balance sheets can be greatly affected by exchange rate fluctuations. Firms need to take seriously how changes in exchange rates can affect their competitiveness. A company with a cost base in a currency that appreciates compared to that of its main foreign competitors may find it more difficult to compete and execute its strategy. Its competitors can utilize such a new-found relative advantage to capture market share by lowering product prices in a way the disadvantaged firm cannot match. Even firms that are purely domestic in their operations, and thus seemingly unexposed to foreign exchange rates, can in fact be exposed through indirect competitive effects and recognize the possibility of being outcompeted in their home market due to an adverse exchange rate change.

Two Stylized Facts About Exchange Rates

The importance of exchange rates to governments and businesses alike should be clear. But what do we know about exchange rates? Given their central role in the financial system, a vast number of studies have been carried out examining the behaviour of exchange rates from various points of view. We will limit ourselves to two stylized facts about them that are of particular relevance to foreign exchange risk management (FXRM) in firms.

1. Changes in exchange rates are largely unpredictable, at least in the short to medium term.
2. Exchange rates can fluctuate significantly over time.

Considerable intellectual firepower has been devoted to the issue of whether exchange rates can be successfully predicted. Why do people think that should be possible in the first place? The idea is that exchange rates, in principle, ought to be determined by fundamental macroeconomic variables such as gross domestic product, aggregate income, interest rates, and trade imbalances. These economic fundamentals are to a fair degree possible to forecast. Hence, one might argue, future exchange rates should also be predictable.

The Law of One Price certainly suggests predictability in exchange rates. This is the idea that, given free trade, exchange rates are set in such a way as to equalize prices of goods and services across different currency regimes.[1] The Big Mac Index, an invention of the London-based magazine *The Economist*, is an application of this logic. The Big Mac is a flagship item on the menu of McDonalds. Because it is standardized and looks more or less the same wherever one goes in the world, its price should, according to the Law of One Price, equalize across borders through the exchange rate. A Big Mac in Oslo, for example, ought to cost the same bought in Norwegian kroner as one in Stockholm,

---

[1] Purchasing Power Parity is an extension of the same principle, except that it applies to a basket of goods rather than a specific item.

multiplied by the NOK/SEK exchange rate. If the hamburger costs 50 Swedish krona in Stockholm and it takes 1.2 krona to buy one Norwegian krone, the model predicts that a hamburger in Oslo costs 41.67 kroner. Then a Swede with 50 Swedish krona can buy a hamburger on either side of the border for his or her money.[2]

Taken as a whole, however, empirical studies have shown that exchange rates are *not* predictable. Meese and Rogoff published an important early study on this subject in 1983. They found that the model that best predicted exchange rates was a simple so-called 'random walk', in which the forecast is set equal to today's exchange rate (the spot rate). In other words, our best guess for what tomorrow's exchange rate is going to be is today's exchange rate. Adding economic fundamentals to the model and using more elaborate econometric techniques did not improve the forecasting ability noticeably. More recent studies have investigated ever more sophisticated algorithms and worked through ever larger quantities of data, yet there is still no leading indicator that reliably and consistently helps us forecast changes in exchange rates.

The fact that we cannot predict changes in exchange rates has an important corollary. It means that a principle in international economics known as the 'International Fisher Effect' does not hold. According to this idea, proposed by economist Irving Fisher, the *expected* change in an exchange rate depends on the difference between the nominal interest rates in the countries concerned. If the yield in the money market for papers with a one-year maturity is 3% in the USA but only 1% in the euro-area, we would expect the US dollar to weaken by approximately 2% over the course of the year. A change in the exchange rate of this size is, according to Fisher's idea, what equalizes the two investment opportunities in the eyes of investors.

Interest rate differentials do not predict future spot rates well, however, at least not in the way envisioned by Fisher. Reflecting

---

[2] As of 31 May 2019, this equilibrium did not hold. On this day, a Big Mac cost 42 Swedish krona, whereas the price in Norway was 42 kroner. The NOK/SEK exchange rate on that day was 1.084. According to *The Economist*'s Big Mac Index, this suggests an 8.4% overvaluation of the Norwegian krone. A forecaster might use this information to predict a weakening of the Norwegian krone.

this fact, historically it has paid off to invest in the higher-yielding currency: you earn a higher interest rate, but the exchange rate does not move enough to offset this gain. This pattern is the basis of the so-called 'carry trade', a trading strategy that involves borrowing money in a low-yield currency (e.g. the Japanese yen) and investing it in a higher-yielding currency (e.g. the Australian dollar). While typically producing consistent gains over significant periods of time, such a strategy comes with an obvious catch: foreign exchange risk. If there is a sudden spike in exchange rate volatility, then many years of small gains can be turned into a major loss.

This brings us to our second stylized fact about exchange rates, namely that they can fluctuate significantly over time. For example, the exchange rate between two of the world's major currencies, the US dollar and the euro, has seen economically very significant fluctuations since the launch of the euro in 1999. In late 2005, the euro was trading at US$1.2, after which the dollar lost in value, reaching US$1.55 in mid-2008. After a strengthening of the dollar during 2009, which sent the exchange rate below US$1.3, the euro again rose back to over US$1.5 in late 2010, only to quickly drop towards US$1.2 again in the early part of 2011. These gyrations mean that either currency can gain or lose 20–30% of its value in a relatively short amount of time. The implications for exporting firms with their cost base largely concentrated in one of these currencies are significant, as their ability to compete and make money is directly affected by such changes.

Why are exchange rates so volatile? To address this question, it should be remembered that currencies are fiat money, which is to say that they are valid by government decree. They have a value basically because we agree that they have one. A distinction can be made between 'paper money' issued at discretion by the country's central bank and money whose value is guaranteed by ultimately being convertible into gold or some other precious metal. Today, currencies are essentially paper money. What is more, since 1973 the exchange rates between most major currencies in the world have been floating rather than fixed. This followed the break-down of the Bretton Woods Agreement, under which other currencies were pegged to the US dollar. Floating exchange rates mean that their values are determined in competitive markets with no or very limited intervention from central banks. Not surprisingly, while the risk of sudden and big shifts due to devaluation of one currency is now less, exchange rates have become more volatile and unpredictable compared to the regimes of fixed exchange rates. Substantial variability in exchange rates is thus an empirical fact, much more so than the rate of change suggested by the fundamentals that supposedly determine exchange rates.

Sometimes the value of a currency collapses almost completely. The Swedish central bank, the Sveriges Riksbank, raised its interest rate to over 500% in a futile attempt to keep the Swedish krona from devaluing in the early 1990s. When the attempt failed, the country was sent into its worst economic crisis since the depression of the 1930s. Another example is the Argentine peso, whose value fell dramatically in 2002 when the government was forced to abandon the fixed exchange rate. Once floated, the peso continued to lose value, which caused extreme difficulties for both the private and public sectors to procure the imports on which they had come to rely.

The broader point is that the value of a fiat currency is a mirror of the trustworthiness of the country's leading institutions, as viewed by the international capital markets. A collapsing currency really only reflects that the capital markets have finally lost faith in the country's leadership and economic policies. Often the fear is that poor policies will create rapid inflation down the road, which erodes the value of a currency. Add to this the fact that there is also a temptation to speculate against currencies that are thought to be on a slippery slope. Speculators like George Soros have brought down currencies through bold trading strategies. The euro, very much a political project, has had its share of naysayers since its very beginnings. The critics have pointed out the inherent instability that comes from having a monetary union without fiscal union, claiming that the euro is doomed to ultimately break down. The US dollar, for its part, also has some dark clouds hanging over it. Due to its large budget deficits and rapidly rising national debt there are, at the end of the 2010s, plenty of commentators who envision a substantial weakening of the dollar and a demise of its role as the world's primary reserve currency. However, it should be noted that this gloomy view of the dollar has been around for at least a decade, and, so far, has been proven wrong. As Warren Buffet has said, betting against the US economy has been a mistake for over 200 years.

Such dramatic declines in the value of a currency can be of a magnitude well beyond any historically 'normal' levels. This makes our innate tendency to foresee reversions of a price to its historical mean somewhat problematic. When a price or rate is trading above or below its historical mean people are often inclined to believe it will move back towards that average ('mean revert'). While a lot of times this is how exchange rates *seem* to behave, the potential for large and permanent shifts in the level cannot be ruled out. There is no economic law that ensures that some long-run average ultimately obtains. The mean level of an exchange rate over time is never guaranteed, for the reasons just discussed. And even when an exchange rate does seem to behave as if it is mean reverting, getting the timing right to profit from changes in exchange rates on a consistent basis is exceedingly difficult.

Where does all this leave us? Our review here suggests that corporate managers should not devote a great deal of resources to producing forecasts. Using very simple models, or even assuming that today's exchange rate is our best guess for the future as well, produces forecasts that are as reasonable as any other. Managers instead should be more attuned to the potential for significant dislocations in the value of an exchange rate. Proactively assessing the downside risk inherent in a particular currency can help avoid situations where the firm is caught unprepared for FX volatility. Which brings us to the topic that will occupy the rest of this book, namely that of understanding corporate exposure to FX risk.

A Definition of FXRM

A simple definition of corporate risk management is managing the *variability* of corporate performance. We build on this definition to define FXRM as managing the impact of changes in exchange rates on corporate performance.

We take the view that FXRM is primarily about managing exposures to exchange rates so as to ensure that threshold levels of performance are met that allow a firm to execute its business strategy optimally. FX exposures, if left unchecked, can derail a firm's competitiveness and ability to achieve attractive profit margins. It can also impair its capacity to undertake value-enhancing investments, or even meet cash commitments related to debt or other liabilities which must be honoured to ensure that the firm's future existence is not in doubt.

We take a comprehensive view of FXRM that does not just focus on the technicalities of managing a specific exposure. Our definition of FXRM spans the following activities:

- Organizing the FX risk management function (centralization vs decentralization).
- Quantifying exposures to FX on various performance metrics (cash flow, net income, balance sheet, financial ratios, etc.).
- Building appropriate decision-support tools addressing FX exposures and policies.
- Formulating a consistent FX risk management policy to guide decision-making.
- Coordinating FXRM with other risk management activities.
- Using risk management techniques to mitigate FX exposures when this is called for (natural hedges, currency composition of debt, derivatives).
- Communicating FX exposures and risk management policies to internal decision-makers and external stakeholders.

This view leaves out the goal of trying to 'beat the market' by speculating on the direction of future changes in exchange rates. It has been documented by academic research that a majority of firms engage in this behaviour, referred to as either 'selective hedging' or 'speculation'. Selective hedging is about adjusting the hedging positions based on market views, whereas speculation is about taking positions in search of financial gain without necessarily hedging an underlying exposure.

For many treasurers, taking a view on interest rates and exchange rates is seen as a natural part of their job of minimizing financing costs. Boards of directors around the globe seem perfectly willing to endorse this activity, to the extent that they even pause to reflect on it at all. Treasurers appear to have a general mandate to use their view on markets to adjust positions that affect the firm's exposure to interest rates and exchange rates.

There is little academic evidence, however, to suggest that managers are successful at timing the markets. Therefore, considering the resources that go into this activity, one might suspect that, on balance, it affects firm value negatively, especially since selective hedging tends to make performance less predictable and transparent. But whether taking market views should be part of the firm's activities is ultimately something for the firm's shareholders, the board, and managers to agree on. We are agnostic on this issue.

The reader interested in how to build models for predicting exchange rates, or developing strategies for beating the market, is instead referred to textbooks on international finance, which cover this topic in some detail. This book leaves this question out altogether, preferring instead to see the future spot rate as largely unpredictable. As previously noted, we suggest that the emphasis is shifted towards understanding the scope for variability in exchange rates, and how that stands to affect the firm's performance and its ability to optimally execute its business plan. A thorough understanding of these mechanisms will increase the likelihood that sound and pro-active FX strategies are implemented that help the firm compete successfully in a wide range of possible scenarios for the future.

Quoting Exchange Rates

In this book, we always quote an exchange rate as units of home currency per one unit of foreign currency. For example, in the exchange rate USD/EUR, the euro is considered the home currency. It should be read as the number of euros needed to buy one dollar, or the price of one dollar in euro terms. Similarly, CHF/EUR is the price of one Swiss franc expressed in euros.[3]

This convention has the implication that a higher value of the exchange rate always means a stronger (i.e. more expensive) foreign currency. For example, if the USD/EUR exchange rate goes from 0.8 to 0.9, this implies a stronger US dollar, because it now takes more euros to buy one dollar. In this context, one would speak of a 12.5% 'appreciation' of the dollar in euro terms. If a currency instead weakens, it is said to 'depreciate'.

Throughout this book, corporate performance is assumed to be measured and communicated in the home currency of the company. We view the home currency as the currency in which the firm being discussed prepares and reports its consolidated financial statements.[4] The term 'functional currency' is used synonymously with home currency.[5] We use the term 'home currency' exclusively to mean the currency used to prepare the *consolidated* financial statements of the entire company. We may sometimes

---

[3] In FX markets, the foreign currency would be referred to as the 'base currency' whereas the home currency would be referred to as the 'price currency' or 'quoted currency'.

[4] Alternatively, the home currency could be understood as the currency of the country in which the firm is incorporated ('statutory currency'). We ignore this aspect here to reduce jargon.

[5] According to International Financial Reporting Standards (IFRS), functional currency is defined as 'the currency of the primary economic environment in which the entity operates' (i.e. the currency in which it carries out the major part of its business transactions). The firm may choose a different 'presentation currency', which is the technical term in this framework for the currency in which the financial statements are reported. We ignore this distinction, however, since functional currency and presentation currency are rarely different in practice.

refer to the functional currency of the firm's foreign subsidiaries as 'foreign currency'.

Our convention implies that the quotation of exchange rates depends on which firm is used in the example. If we are talking about a German manufacturer, then the home currency would be the euro and the exchange rate is quoted as USD/EUR. In contrast, if the perspective is that of a US exporter, the home currency is the US dollar and the exchange rate would be quoted as EUR/USD.

Quoting exchange rates based on how the firm measures its performance leads to a more unified approach. When modelling corporate performance analytically, an exchange rate thus quoted immediately informs us about the home currency value of expected cash flows in foreign currency: just multiply the amount of foreign currency and the exchange rate. It is furthermore less likely to lead to confusion compared to using some arbitrary norm established by participants in the FX markets.[6] The financial analysis of the firm's performance is made more difficult if the same currency alternatively appears in the numerator and the denominator, depending on which currency pair we are talking about.

A basis point is 1/100 of one percentage point. It therefore refers to the fourth decimal in a quoted exchange rate. For example, if the USD/EUR is 0.8522 and increases by 1 basis point, the new exchange rate is 0.8523.

Outline of the Book

The presumption of much of the literature on risk management is that managing variability helps ensure that corporate objectives are met and value is enhanced. We cover the arguments according to which FXRM may create value, which revolve around identifying and eliminating various negative consequences of variability in performance (Chapter 1).

---

[6] There is a norm among actors in the FX markets and data providers such as Bloomberg that dictates a certain hierarchy concerning which is the base and price currency for any given pair. For example, the Swedish krona would, by this convention, always be quoted as the price currency against the US dollar, but normally not the other way around.

A firm is exposed to exchange rate risk if its performance is sensitive to fluctuations in the value of one or more currencies relative to another currency. Most firms of a non-trivial size are in one way or other exposed to exchange rates. These exposures can be straightforward, such as those arising from converting revenue or costs in foreign currencies into home currency, or more subtle and indirect effects, such as those resulting from changes in competitiveness or in the general demand for the firm's products (Chapter 2).

Corporate exposure to FX also includes the effects of exchange rates on financial statements from translation effects and fair value accounting. Focusing on the economics of a hedging decision is not enough for an effective FX risk manager. There are multiple impacts on performance measures that arise from the need to translate assets and liabilities denominated in a foreign currency. It is essential to understand these mechanisms in order to avoid surprises and protect important objectives (Chapters 3 and 4).

Once the exposures are understood and quantified, there are several ways of managing FX risk in a firm. Derivatives have the potential to reduce variability when their exposures partly or wholly offset those arising from the firm's commercial activities. Firms today can choose from an impressive array of financial instruments that can be used for this purpose (Chapter 5).

Derivatives offer firms a great deal of flexibility in terms of choosing a particular risk–return profile. However, the way these instruments are accounted for has created a headache for many corporates. It turns out that unrealized gains and losses from derivatives can lead to situations where volatility in net income is higher, not lower. Hedge accounting has been offered as a way of keeping these unwanted fluctuations out of the bottom line, but comes with its own disadvantages. Having a working knowledge of these issues helps the FX manager navigate the hedging decision (Chapter 6).

The FXRM function can be organized in different ways. One important aspect is whether the management of FXRM is centralized or not. Business units may have what appears to be a legitimate claim to manage their own risks, but there are also significant benefits of centralization from the corporate perspective (Chapter 7).

Integrated risk management is a strong trend. Centralizing FXRM does not guarantee that integrated risk management follows. Rather, this calls for setting FX policy in a broader context, where risk is assessed on a 'portfolio basis' (i.e. jointly with other risk exposures), as well as relating this variability to corporate objectives like the successful implementation of the business plan (Chapter 8).

There then follows a chapter that ties together the insights from the previous chapters into a practical framework for managing FX risk. The emphasis here is on developing strategies for value-enhancing FXRM. We point to the importance of having a decision-support tool that accurately reflects the firm's exposures to FX on various levels of performance (Chapter 9).

The final chapter of the book discusses how to communicate FXRM. This communication takes place on two fronts: externally, towards analysts and investors, and internally, towards the firm's senior decision-makers. The purpose of external communication is to achieve optimal transparency and a lower cost of capital, whereas the purpose of internal communication is improved decision-making (Chapter 10).

Further Reading

Adam, T. R. and C. S. Fernando. 2006. Hedging, speculation, and shareholder value. *Journal of Financial Economics* **81**, 283–309.

Meese, R. A. and K. Rogoff. 1983. Empirical exchange rate models of the seventies: Do they fit out of sample? *Journal of International Economics* **14**, 3–24.

Chapter 1

Why Manage Foreign Exchange Risk?

O ne of the more puzzling questions facing corporate management is the risk management decision. This is about deciding whether to use a company's resources to actively try to reduce risk, here understood as variability in corporate performance. Our focus in this chapter is therefore to understand when it makes sense for a firm to reduce variability in its performance through managing its FX exposures. Why would a firm be better off managing risk than just accepting its exposures as part of doing business?

To fix our ideas, we can take hedging as a proxy for corporate risk management. Hedging is the use of financial derivatives to alter a firm's exposure to a specific market risk. Many other forms of risk management are possible, like buying insurance, operational risk mitigation, relying on equity rather than debt financing, and keeping a buffer of cash to deal with adverse outcomes. We will in fact emphasize that hedging, while highly flexible, is for the most part only able to address relatively near-term exposures (more on this in Chapter 9). By changing the currency exposure at an operational level (i.e. actively trying to net out cash inflows and cash outflows), or by borrowing long term in foreign currency, the firm is likely to achieve more durable reductions in FX risk.

Focusing on hedging for now, however, allows us to keep the terminology brief and tap into a rich literature that has developed on why firms should hedge their exposures. Most of the arguments developed in this chapter transfer over to other forms of risk management.

The business case for hedging is far from obvious. In some companies, questions like 'Why should we hedge?' and 'Should we hedge cash flows or earnings?' never seem to get fully settled. The issues are raised, meetings are held, memos are written, and policy documents established. Only for the question to get raised again a couple of years later, prompting new discussions and memos in what seems an endless cycle. A clear and robust answer to these questions continues to elude many companies.

Why is it so difficult to pin down why and when firms should use hedging? We are convinced that part of the difficulty lies in the fact that there is an almost infinite number of performance measures that potentially *could* be hedged. For most of these, a plausible-sounding argument to reduce variability can be developed quite easily, because managers are naturally averse to risk and need little convincing that variability in performance, however measured, is 'bad'. For example, it is not uncommon for business units and investment projects to be evaluated based on their operating margin. For the people involved in these projects, 'protecting' these margins through hedging may seem perfectly logical and desirable. Seeing currency fluctuations eat away at the margins, perhaps even causing them to turn negative, can be a terrifying prospect. The desire to protect margins is behind a large number of hedging proposals that are sent further up the corporate system for management, and sometimes even the board of directors, to decide on. So, what should they say to such proposals? Based on what principles?

In what follows we review the arguments in favour of corporate hedging. The goal is to develop a hedging policy that guides management's decision-making, where a plausible case can be made that the advantages of hedging outweigh the disadvantages.

The alternative to a unified hedging policy, we argue, is an ad-hoc approach at least partly captured by different local agendas, pushing for the hedging of specific business projects, which only serves to make hedging incoherent and unpredictable.

From Individual Risk Management to Corporate Risk Management

In trying to come up with some suggestions for what can constitute a basis for a hedging policy in firms, one might consult the academic thinking on the topic. Academic finance has for several decades been analysing the circumstances in which hedging creates value for a firm.

In the literature, the hedging decision of the firm is sometimes contrasted with that of the individual trader or investor. When we are dealing with an individual it comes down to one thing: risk preferences. Why? Because the situation concerns an individual who makes decisions affecting *his or her own* expected wealth and risk. Therefore, it comes down to what you are comfortable with as an individual. Some people do not like risk and prefer a safer alternative. They are the 'risk-averse' individuals who may prefer to hedge as much as they can. Other people are more tolerant of risk. They may consider it fine to retain certain exposures to risk so long as they also get a reward in the form of a commensurate upside potential. Still others may be positively 'risk-loving'. They are the kind of people willing to take significant risks for the pleasure of the thrill.

The broader point here is that for individuals, the hedging decision follows risk preferences. Once the odds and the range of potential outcomes are known, it all depends on this parameter.

Unfortunately, the model for decision-making based on personal risk preferences does not carry over to firms. This is true despite the fact that businesses are run by people. One might think that risk-averse managers will hedge more and risk-seeking ones less, and that is it. But this does not provide a robust business case for hedging. Managers are in fact hired by the owners of a firm to run its operations on a daily basis. In more formal language, they are agents hired by a principal. According to corporation law, the managers and directors of the firm are obliged to use their decision-making powers in the 'best interest of the firm'. This pretty much rules out using managers' own feelings and sentiments about risk as a justification for risk management decisions.

Instead we need to think about how hedging can promote the best interest of the firm. Phrased a bit differently, this is the question of how hedging can increase shareholder value. It changes the question from 'How do we feel about this risk?' to 'How can we demonstrate that shareholders are expected to be better off with this hedge than without it?' This is a much trickier question to answer.

The Case for FXRM: Cash Flow Hedging

The basic thing achieved by a hedge, if correctly executed, is to reduce variability in corporate performance. Let us for now take performance to mean cash flow. This is the metric favoured by academics due to its close relation to firm value, which is given by the discounted value of future free cash flow. Reducing variability in cash flow by itself falls short, however, of presenting a convincing business case for hedging. Why? The answer lies in the symmetric impact of hedging on cash flow variability. Say that we enter an FX hedge, which lowers our maximum loss by US$20 mn. The symmetry of a forward contract implies that we also lower our maximum gain by US$20 mn. A firm that protects itself against unfavourable scenarios has to accept that it misses out on the windfall it would have received in more favourable scenarios. The expected value of such a hedge is zero (or even negative, if there are transaction costs). So, while reducing variability might be 'nice' to some of the managers involved, this is not enough to build a case for hedging.

We can conclude, then, that simply achieving a narrower range of potential outcomes for cash flow does not justify corporate risk management. Instead, theorists have sought to build the case by looking for asymmetries in the way corporate performance is affected by hedging. Hedging can be valuable when there is a negative consequence from cash flow falling below a certain threshold *and* there is no corresponding positive side-effect at high levels of cash flow. Hedging, by reducing the probability of cash flow dropping below the threshold level, reduces the expected cost of these negative consequences. This, in a nutshell, is the idea behind corporate hedging in academic models.

What are the negative consequences that could happen in low-cash-flow scenarios? It is straightforward. Firms need money to meet important cash commitments, like investing in new projects and paying interest and instalments on loans. There are many other commitments to various stakeholders that also require liquidity, like dividends and pension obligations. When a firm does not generate enough cash flow internally, it may not be able to service these cash commitments. Falling below this threshold usually implies some sort of negative consequence. If the firm cannot invest optimally, it will end up being less competitive. If it defaults on its interest payments, it will be sent into bankruptcy. If it sells assets in a fire sale, it may have to accept a price below the assets' fair value. If it cuts back the dividend, shareholders will grumble and reassess the firm's future prospects.

We have now identified the asymmetry we needed. The firm suffers various negative consequences when it fails to reach a certain threshold level of cash flow, but there are no positive consequences, beyond the pure monetary gain, when cash flow is higher than expected. In the good scenarios the surplus cash flows will simply accumulate as more cash.

Someone might reply that it does not matter if cash flow falls below the threshold level because the firm can always borrow to cover up the difference. There might be a credit line it can draw on, or it might have unused borrowing capacity to mitigate the consequences of cash flow shortfalls. Such untapped resources will obviously have to be considered. But all they really do is move the threshold level of performance. With spare debt capacity and cash buffers the firm can tolerate larger cash flow shortfalls. But at some point, the opportunities to get external funding at a reasonable cost will be used up. Creditors will worry about the risks involved, and may suspect that managers will engage in excessive risk-taking. These things push up the cost of debt, and financially weak firms may find themselves shut out of the credit markets altogether. Equity financing provides no easy escape, as the issuing costs are substantial and investors demand a large risk premium. In these circumstances, the availability of operating cash flow plays a crucial role in terms of being able to execute the business plan and meet various cash commitments.

To summarize, the academic literature recommends looking for different threshold levels of cash flow performance where different negative consequences would be triggered. This is a test to which all hedging proposals should be subjected. The question to be asked is: 'Would implementing this hedge, in a meaningful way, reduce the probability that cash flow ends up below the threshold level given by our cash commitments?' This question raises the bar significantly compared to hedging to protect operating margins, or simply locking in a 'good' FX rate.

The Case for FXRM: Protecting Financial Ratios

In academic finance, cash flow has the highest pedigree because of its close relationship with firm value. However, corporate performance is more multifaceted in real life. Realistically, more things will matter than cash flow. Once we acknowledge this, things get more subtle and subjective, but the arguments are worth taking seriously.

One way to motivate FXRM is to say that a particular financial ratio needs to be stabilized, or 'protected'. Some firms have a stated objective that, for example, the debt-to-equity ratio should not go above 0.7. Since both debt and equity are exposed to FX translation gains and losses, it may decide to manage its composition of assets and liabilities in such a way that the probability of exceeding this target is minimized. This is an argument for FXRM that is not uncommon in practice. Granted, maintaining a set of target ratios over time gives a sense of direction and an impression that management is on top of things. But what is there to say that defending a particular ratio actually translates into higher shareholder value? Being a corporate objective by itself does not justify using resources to protect it. An objective is a fairly arbitrary thing, and may not always be connected to shareholder value in an obvious way.

Defining threshold levels of performance in terms of financial ratios can be more easily motivated if breaching them is clearly connected to a negative consequence. Again, we are looking for some asymmetry in the outcome distribution. One way this could happen is if the firm has agreed to a covenant as part of its loan agreement. A covenant is a way for a bank to monitor the firm and decrease the risk of default. If breached, the covenant gives the bank increased legal powers to demand specific actions, or even take control of the firm's policies. Most covenants are financial (i.e. they make reference to financial ratios), and they are usually explicit about the threshold level at which the covenant would be considered violated. This allows firms with financial covenants a clear reference point to use in FXRM.

Another case of financial ratios-based risk management concerns the risk of being downgraded by credit rating agencies. Defending a specific rating is high on the agenda in some companies. Managers may consider it likely that the firm's rating will be downgraded if a particular ratio were to be breached. Hedging can in some cases be used to avoid scenarios involving such breaches of key financial ratios. The major credit rating agencies publish a great deal of information about average ratios associated with their different rating levels. Firms can infer from such tables that level of performance at which they would be at risk of losing their desired rating. For example, according to Moody's rating agency, the average ratio of Funds-From-Operations to Debt of an A-rated company is 34.1%.[1] If a firm wishes to defend its A-rating it should probably not go below this level for any extended period of time.

---

[1] As per the report *Moody's Financial Metrics™ Key Ratios by Rating and Industry for Global Non-Financial Corporates: December 2016* (Moody's, 2017).

Financial ratios therefore provide firms with a potential ref-erence point for understanding what constitutes a critical level of performance. Exchange rates are, as we shall discuss in later chapters, capable of having a substantial impact on financial ratios, not just because of how they affect operating performance but also due to the translation of assets and liabilities from foreign to home currency.

The connection to shareholder value, however, is less obvious for financial ratios than cash flow shortfalls. It is clear that the firm's creditors will applaud any form of risk management that reduces downside risk because it makes debt safer. But maximizing value for debt-holders is not the purpose of corporate management. In fact, due to limited liability, equity-holders enjoy protection from losses beyond the size of their initial investment (i.e. they can simply walk away in a bankruptcy). This feature means that shareholders, at least in certain specific circumstances, take a very different view on risk-taking than creditors. They may even have incentives to bet the house by massively increasing risk (referred to in the literature as 'risk-shifting'). So perhaps defending financial ratios at all costs is mostly doing creditors a favour, but shareholders a disservice?

In most cases, however, it would seem that the interests of shareholders and debt-holders coincide with respect to financial ratios-based FXRM. It is usually a bad outcome also for share-holders if a covenant is violated and banks increase their control over operating policies, for example, by making demands that force management to cut back investments or issue new equity. If a rating downgrade occurs, it may reflect badly on management and increase the firm's borrowing costs. Higher borrowing costs in turn translate into lower shareholder value. The kind of situation where the owners would like to gamble and take a huge risk, knowing that they enjoy limited liability, are, though popular in academic models, a rare occurrence in real life. For the most part shareholders want to keep the firm going and enjoy good relations with the firm's creditors.

Based on the above, we conclude that managing the firm's FX exposures so as to lower the probability of breaching important financial ratio thresholds can many times be justified. It is another matter if management decides to adjust all sorts of policies in order to defend a rating. If the firm purposefully avoids making investments and acquisitions that it thinks are value-creating for the sole purpose of maintaining a certain rating, it could indeed be doing shareholders a disservice. But this is a bigger issue that falls outside FXRM, so we do not pursue it further here.

The Case for FXRM: Managing Net Income Variability

Next, we consider a third dimension of corporate performance, namely earnings-based measures. We may also speak of 'margin-based' measures more generally as firms keep track of their income on several levels: gross profit (revenue less cost of sales), operating profit (gross profit less operating expenses), and various adjusted measures of 'core profits', to give some examples. The firm's ultimate bottom line is of course net income (also called earnings), the measure of profit and loss communicated at great fanfare to the rest of the world every quarter. Net income often attracts massive interest and commentary in the press, and therefore naturally becomes a key concern for management teams.

Does managing variability in net income present a case for FXRM? This is a complicated question that has not been fully resolved. Two camps seem to exist. One argues that yes, protecting against 'bad outcomes' for net income is a valid goal, because it is so important and followed so closely by analysts and investors. If the firm delivers a poor result, or fails to meet expectations, it will immediately get punished and receive a lower valuation. The second camp argues that no, net income is such an arbitrary and accounting-based measure anyway that it does not make sense to make it the centrepiece of a risk management effort. Add to this the fact that management can greatly influence the numbers through the assumptions they are allowed to make in the process of preparing financial statements. Analysts only care about the core operating profits anyway, so any gains and losses from derivatives are just 'noise' that they adjust away.

We argue that it is possible to find instances supporting both views, but that the bulk of the evidence supports the latter. There is indeed a rock-hard focus on underlying operating performance. Recently, for example, a Scandinavian large-cap company reported a foreign-exchange-induced loss in its financial expenses that was almost four times the size of its operating profit. While this appeared to be a serious situation, a striking thing about it was that it was received by analysts with what seemed like indifference. As they are trained to do in business schools, the analysts move such gains and losses out of their preferred measure of operating performance, considering them temporary effects that are not informative about the firm's future prospects.

Does the argument that the firm gets punished for large unexpected losses, and that FXRM can help avoid this, really have any traction? It is actually fully to be expected that the market rethinks its view about a company when it reports a larger-than-expected loss. In light of the newly published quarterly report, the market will reconsider the firm's outlook because the report contains information the market previously did not have. This is in fact normal procedure and how reasonably efficient markets are supposed to operate.

The key question is *how* the market prices in the new information. Let's say the firm's income before financial items is US$200 mn lower than anticipated but there is also a gain on an FX derivative of US$100 mn offsetting the lower operating performance. Will the market price the firm according to a multiple of its operating income or its net income? The latter ratio is the famous price-to-earnings multiple, probably the most widely used multiple out there. If market participants price the firm as a multiple of net income, the derivative gain will get capitalized into the price by the same multiple as operating income. In that case hedging will indeed stabilize the value of the firm. But it is not reasonable that the market prices the firm's earnings in this way. Capitalizing the derivative gain with the same multiple implies that it is expected to generate the same gain in all quarters going forward, which is clearly not realistic. The effect of a derivative is limited to its expiry date, and the present value of *future* hedging transactions is zero. Instead, it is much more likely that analysts see this as a temporary effect that does not affect the firm's future prospects. That is, it prices the firm according to its view of underlying operating performance.

Proponents of earnings-based FXRM to protect and stabilize net income need to rely on subtler arguments. Perhaps investors just do not 'like' net income volatility on a more general level? If so, they will pay a premium on stocks whose earnings are more stable, even though the expected mean is the same. The claim that there is a risk premium on net income variability is precarious in light of existing theory about how assets are priced. But many managers seem to believe it nonetheless, as evidenced by the extent to which they engage in 'earnings management', that is to say making convenient assumptions regarding the value of its assets and liabilities to smooth net income. A legendary case in point is General Electric, who under Jack Welsh's leadership presented growing net income from continuing operations in 100 consecutive quarters.[2] Throughout this period, core earnings (i.e. net income adjusted for managerial discretion) were lower and much bumpier. According to many academics in finance, earnings management is based on 'market myths' (i.e. a false and simplistic belief about how the market prices the firm's stock).

The case for earnings-based FXRM thus rests on shaky academic grounds. But it is hard to entirely discount the possibility that in some situations it makes sense to reduce variability in net income. The crucial issue as far as FXRM is concerned is whether different external stakeholders make decisions that affect the firm based on its net income performance, and whether those decisions can be swayed in a favourable direction by FXRM.

As before, we need to look for negative and asymmetric consequences of net income volatility to defend net-income-based risk management. Perhaps the firm is under a lot of pressure to

---

[2] See Roger Lowenstein's book *Origins of the Crash: The Great Bubble and its Undoing* (Penguin Books, 2004) for a full account.

improve its performance and analysts are losing their faith in the management team's ability to run the business. Perhaps also its financiers are paying a lot of attention to how its net income develops, and that their willingness to provide additional funding depends on net income not falling below some reference level. This could be a very unwelcome time for the firm to experience FX-related losses. FXRM could then be valuable to the extent that it reduces the risk that net income falls below the perceived threshold value where the investors would conclude that the firm is a hopeless case and withdraw their financing. While this setting is not entirely inconceivable, it does depend on several fairly strong assumptions, like investors following simplistic decision rules with regard to net income performance. The burden of proof in cases like these should lie on the individual(s) who argue in favour of hedging on these grounds.

Key Chapter Takeaways

➢ Risk management (i.e. reducing variability in corporate performance) does not automatically translate into higher shareholder value.
➢ Managers' dislike of risk and performance variability does not constitute a sufficient business case for FXRM.
➢ Academic models of value-enhancing risk management are built on the idea that there is an asymmetry: poor performance triggers a negative and costly consequence, but good performance only leads to more cash accumulating.
➢ Negative consequences of cash flow variability include not being able to invest optimally or maintain dividends; a failure to meet interest payments; or having to make asset fire sales.
➢ Managing the risk that cash flow falls short of important cash commitments presents the strongest argument in favour of FXRM.

➤ FXRM can also be justified on the grounds that it makes breaching key performance thresholds for financial ratios less likely, for example, related to loan covenants or credit ratings.
➤ Stabilizing earnings, or some other profit margin, tends to be the weakest argument for FXRM and must be critically assessed before being accepted.

Further Reading

Froot, K. A., D. S. Scharfstein, and J. C. Stein. 1994. A framework for risk management. *Harvard Business Review* **72**, 91–102.

Smith, C. W. and R. M. Stulz. 1985. The determinants of firms' hedging policies. *Journal of Financial and Quantitative Analysis* **20**, 391–405.

Chapter 2
Commercial Exposure to FX

T he previous chapter established a basic approach to FXRM: that is, managing FX exposures so as to keep the risk of breaching critical threshold levels of performance acceptably low. Regardless of which performance metric is ultimately chosen, a keen understanding of the firm's exposure to risk is a prerequisite for being successful at this task.

A good place to start in the quest for a solid understanding of how performance relates to exchange rates is the firm's commercial exposure. In our usage of the term, commercial exposure is largely synonymous with the exposure on cash flow generated through its various business activities, or its operating cash flow. At this point we leave out financial and temporary effects such as those generated by asset sales or other restructurings. Our interest lies in the core operating performance of the firm, which is to say its revenue and the costs it incurs in the process of generating that revenue. Most of the other tasks in FXRM become much more difficult, or even meaningless, if the firm's commercial exposure is poorly understood. In many ways, a firm constructs its portfolio of derivatives and debt instruments so that the exposures on these items balance out those resulting from the commercial activities.

Therefore, there is hardly any basis for making FXRM decisions if this crucial piece of information is lacking.

This chapter describes concepts and methods that can be used in quantifying a firm's commercial exposure to exchange rates. As will become evident, while straightforward in principle, quantification is often a formidable challenge in practice. Managers regularly cite frustration with the quality of exposure information as a top reason for lack of progress in FXRM. To remedy this, we point to the need for a consistent methodology that targets the relevant aspects of corporate performance. Managers must also be willing to abandon the comfort of the familiar and easily observable – which is to say near-term receivables and payables – for a broader and more strategic view of its exposure to FX.

The Basics of Transaction Exposure

A firm that sells all its products in its home market, and that sources all of its parts and materials domestically, is unlikely to worry much about FX risk. True, indirectly one or more of its cost elements may be affected by exchange rates somewhere in the supply chain, and some percentage of that may be passed on to the firm in the form of higher prices. But such effects would normally be viewed as either being of limited concern, or beyond the firm's ability to influence, and therefore largely off the minds of its managers.

FX risk typically becomes a serious point on the management agenda once the firm initiates exports, or begins a relationship with a supplier in another country. An exporting firm will, for practical reasons, in most cases need to quote the product's price in the foreign currency. That is, the sales generated from exports are normally in foreign currency. But they need not be, and we will come back to this possibility.

Exposures that arise in connection with commercial deals are usually referred to as 'transaction exposure'. The different phases of a transaction exposure are illustrated in Figure 2.1. When they hear the term transaction exposure, most people think of the receivable

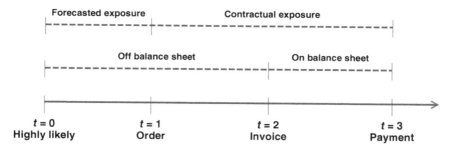

Figure 2.1 Transaction exposure

or payable that is created when the product is invoiced. From an economic point of view, however, the exposure actually begins already when the transaction is highly likely. A Swedish exporter, for example, may have had a successful sales pitch with a German manufacturer, and there is a clear understanding that orders are forthcoming. At first ($t = 0$ in Figure 2.1) the exposure is only forecasted, but because it is highly likely to occur, a case could be made for managing the exposure already at this point.

When the order is placed ($t = 1$ in Figure 2.1), the deal is done. While there may be some contingencies and uncertainties related to the production (and delivery), at this point the exposure should be rather clear in that the firm knows how much it will invoice and when payment is due. The exporter in our example knows that it can look forward to receiving a payment of a certain size on a certain date, provided that it successfully delivers the product according to the terms. The date of payment should be reasonably clear too, because credit terms are negotiated as part of the deal, or simply follow conventions in the industry.

The transaction finally enters the balance sheet (i.e. becomes a receivable or payable) when the product is delivered and the invoice created ($t = 2$ in Figure 2.1). This is the 'event' that accountants require for formally recognizing a transaction and showing it in the books. The transaction has now been monetized in the sense that there is a fixed quantity of currency units due for payment. For the Swedish exporter this means that a sale has been recognized and a euro-denominated trade receivable created. If we ignore the possibility that the German customer fails to make good on its obligations, the only uncertainty remaining at this point is the Swedish krona value of this receivable when it is due for payment. Because the future EUR/SEK exchange rate is uncertain, so will be the final quantity of Swedish krona that the exporter realizes from the deal. This is the point at which the question of whether to hedge arises in many companies. By entering a forward sale with a financial institution, the firm can eliminate uncertainty about the final krona value of the receivable at the maturity date and effectively 'lock in' the prevailing forward rate.

Forecasting Net Exposures

In industries where sales orders are few but large, firms may approach transaction exposures in a sequence similar to the one outlined in the previous section. Each deal is so important for the corporate bottom line that they are managed on a case-by-case basis. In other firms there is more of a steady stream of deals, too numerous for each to be micro-managed. When that is the situation, managers need to approach the management of commercial FX exposures a bit differently.

Let us say that our Swedish exporter expands and finds new customers across the euro-area. Now there is a continuous flow of euro-denominated receivables being created and settled throughout the year. The challenge is to aggregate this flow up to a manageable quantity that summarizes the firm's exposure to the EUR/SEK exchange rate. If the volume of business is steady, the number of euros coming in over a specific time period can simply be summed up. Perhaps the firm's records show that on average each month the firm generates sales of €120 mn, and managers are willing to assume this is also a good forecast for the coming 12-month period. Then they know that, on a yearly basis, the firm has to translate roughly €1.5 bn into Swedish krona. So, by forecasting its commercial activities, the firm has created a basis for managing its overall exposure to the euro. This is referred to as 'anticipated transaction exposure'.

Now, rather than looking at a specific receivable, we have defined exposure in terms of the anticipated volume of euro-denominated business over a whole year. While focusing on a specific receivable offers the comfort of seeming exactness and precision, obviously the volume of business over a year is a much more relevant dimension as far as the firm's actual performance and financial health is concerned.

In fact, switching from a focus on individual transactions to framing exposures in terms of forecasted volumes of business is one of the most important transitions in FXRM. Hedging of innumerable small transactions makes little economic sense as the FX rate applied by the bank normally reflects the size of the transaction. That is, the larger the transaction volume, the more attractive the terms the bank can offer because of the increased negotiating power of the firm.[1] In addition, a multitude of smaller transactions increases administrative costs in the firm.

Managing exposures on a transaction-by-transaction basis also gives rise to inefficiencies in cases where the firm has many business units that carry out transactions in the same currency. One business unit may be hedging a receivable in US dollars while another unit simultaneously hedges a payable in that currency. To save on the spreads between selling and buying rates that come with each hedging transaction, exposures should first be netted. For example, a Norwegian firm in which two business areas simultaneously cover a US$10 mn exposure (one buying and one selling dollars) would incur transaction costs of 30,000 kroner (US$3,509), assuming a USD/NOK exchange rate of 8.55 and a modest bid–ask spread of 30 basis points.

---

[1] This is true up to a certain point. A large enough hedging transaction may constitute too large a credit risk for the bank that is the counterparty, which would affect the bid–ask spread negatively. Also, for some smaller currencies, derivative transactions above a certain size may actually affect the exchange rate itself. We discuss hedging strategies in more detail in Chapter 9.

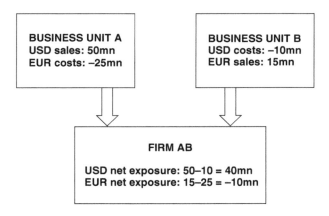

Figure 2.2 Netting exposures

Netting exposures is a core principle of FXRM. When a firm has costs as well as revenues in a given currency, it is said to be 'naturally hedged'. The firm's net exposure is revenue less cost in a particular currency. The net can of course be either positive or negative, depending on which side dominates. The important thing is that the firm is diligent in analysing its currency exposure on both the revenue and the cost side so as to utilize any natural hedges that may exist. Figure 2.2 illustrates a simple netting procedure in a firm that consists of two business units with commercial activities exposing it to two different currencies.

A Simple Model of Commercial Exposure

A firm dealing with anticipated transaction exposures may find it easier to quantify their overall exposure with the help of a model. The estimate of total operating cash flow can be built up from various projected cash flows in different currencies. Such a model would identify the exposures both on the revenue and the cost side of the business to arrive at a net exposure. Our Swedish exporter may look for any euro-denominated fixed or variable costs that offset its revenue in that currency.

$$CF_{SEK} = Q * P_{EUR} * XR - Q * VC_{EUR} * XR - FC_{EUR} * XR \quad (2.1)$$

In Eq. (2.1), CF_{SEK} is the cash flow measured in Swedish krona; Q is the volume of sales (number of units sold); P is the average sales price obtained on these units sold, measured in euros; XR is the EUR/SEK exchange rate; VC_{EUR} is the unit variable cost, measured in euros; FC_{EUR} is the fixed cost, measured in euros.

A model of cash flow such as Eq. (2.1) can be used to derive an estimate of the firm's net exposure to each exchange rate. This is done by first separating out the exchange rate:

$$CF_{SEK} = XR * (Q * P_{EUR} - Q * VC_{EUR} - FC_{EUR}) \quad (2.2)$$

The expression in brackets in Eq. (2.2) gives the firm's exposure to the EUR/SEK exchange rate. As can be seen, the volume of units sold is a key determinant of exposure. If the Swedish exporter in our example has its cost base entirely in the home currency, and it does not source any of its raw materials in euros, then the last two terms drop out, leaving the firm's net exposure defined as $(Q * P_{EUR})$. The more units that are sold, the more foreign currency the firm will have to exchange for the home currency. Likewise, the higher the product price, all else being equal, the more foreign currency the firm will have to exchange.

At this point we have identified two crucial elements determining a firm's commercial exposure to FX: volume of units sold and product price (stated in foreign currency). As long as somebody is willing to make a forecast of these items, the firm has a basis for calculating its net exposure, which can subsequently form the basis for FXRM decisions. Making such forecasts is typically a part of the firm's budgeting process, so what we need to add is the requirement that the forecast is done on a per-currency basis. As part of the budgeting process the firm would also identify the extent to which its cost base is in foreign currency. Doing so, any 'natural hedges' are accounted for and the firm can focus on managing the resulting net exposure.

Competitive Exposures

Up to now we have been dealing with a simplified picture: transaction exposures arising from exports to another country with a currency different than the home currency. As the company generates foreign currency, it needs to exchange that into its home currency, which is what creates a transaction exposure.

The reality of FX exposure, however, is much more muddled and complex for most firms operating internationally. This is not just because they are dealing with more than one currency. If the situation is as straightforward as in our example, adding more currencies does not make the analysis markedly more complicated. It is just more of the same. Instead, it gets complicated because commercial exposure to FX is more dynamic than is often recognized, to the point where it defies attempts to capture it in bottom-up projections as part of a budgeting process.

What do we mean when we say that commercial exposures to FX are 'dynamic'? The answer is that Q and P in Eq. (2.2) are not independent of XR. That is, the exchange rate influences the other variables in the model. This tends to happen because firms operate in competitive markets, forever battling it out in a search for market share and volume growth. The price that firms set for their product is an important lever in this game. The price is often directly influenced by one or more exchange rates (through mechanisms we will explore below). The price, in turn, affects what kind of sales volumes the firm is able to realize. As is well known, the higher the price, the lower the number of units one can expect to sell in a competitive market. Formally:

$$\mathrm{CF_{SEK}} = Q(P) * P(\mathrm{XR}) * \mathrm{XR} \tag{2.3}$$

The meaning of Eq. (2.3) is that the price is a function of the exchange rate, and the sales volume is in turn a function of the price. The three elements making up commercial cash flow are therefore tied together by the firm's pricing strategy. This is the essence of competitive exposure, which is a well-known yet elusive concept.

To see how it works, we need to go back to the situation of our Swedish exporter. It will set a price that ensures it achieves a certain level of profitability on each deal, yet also creates a high enough demand for its product. This is classic economics: setting the price high maximizes the return on the deals that get made, but will scare off some customers and may leave the firm's factories running at below capacity. A Swedish firm exporting to a euro-based country will most likely, for its own budget purposes, have a list price for its products framed in Swedish krona to decide what is an attractive profit margin. It then has to decide how to approach its export market. It would normally quote its German customers a price in euros. Initially, this can be a simple matter of restating its list price in euro terms using the prevailing EUR/SEK exchange rate. The sales it anticipates for the year, measured in the home currency, will be based on this price and the forecasted exchange rate.

Going forward, however, the exchange rate is highly likely to fluctuate. Let us say that our exporter has some luck in that the euro strengthens, perhaps from 9 to 9.15. It decides to keep the price in euros unchanged, so that German customers see the same product price as before. An unchanged price in foreign currency (euros) means that realized sales volumes will remain close to the original forecast. There is, however, a beneficial effect from using the new and higher exchange rate when converting the stream of euros back into the home currency. The firm experiences an economic windfall thanks to the stronger euro.

The exporter has an option, however, which is to lower the euro price of its products. Because of the stronger euro, it can afford to set a lower price, yet continue to meet its budgeted level of profitability in home currency terms. In this case, the windfall comes about because of higher sales volumes compared to those in the budget. The firm may be calculating that its German-based competitors cannot match the price decrease because they have a different cost base. Their operating costs are all in euros, so they are not experiencing a positive effect from the stronger euro. These firms may have very limited opportunities to follow the price cut, because any such cut would immediately chip away at their margins.

Exactly how much the Swedish exporter's sales will respond to an unmatched price cut depends on the price sensitivity of its potential customers. Whether price is a big factor or not depends on the industry in question. If an industry is characterized by long-term relationships and a high degree of product differentiation, there may not be much scope for capturing new market share through opportunistic pricing. If the industry leans towards bulk and competition through price, there may be more of an impact.

It is often a challenge to quantify these kinds of competitive exposures in bottom-up projections in spreadsheets. Firms should, however, carefully analyse whether the preconditions for FX-induced competitive dynamics exist in order to better appreciate the full range of potential outcomes for different scenarios of exchange rates. This process begins with a fundamental analysis of the firm and its closest competitors. It involves working through a series of questions that target the competitive structure of the industry. Some of the questions to be addressed are listed in Box 2.1.

Box 2.1   Fundamental analysis of competitive exposure

Where are our main production facilities located?

In which currency are we sourcing our input factors?

Where are the main production facilities of our key competitors located?

In which currency are our key competitors sourcing their input factors?

How sensitive are customers to changes in product price?

How likely are our competitors to respond tit-for-tat to changes in the price?

What are our operating margins and those of our key competitors?

After contemplating questions such as those in Box 2.1, the Swedish exporter in our example concludes that indeed its main competitors have a cost base largely in euros. It also estimates that these competitors operate with modest profit margins, suggesting that they would find it difficult to match any price cuts. A review of the customer base in Germany and other euro countries indicates that customers historically have been quite sensitive to price.[2] Such insights from a fundamental analysis, together with an analysis of industry sales figures in the past, leads the managers to conclude that, as a rule of thumb, a 5% decrease in the sales price would boost sales volumes by 3%. Of course, what it gains when the euro strengthens, it loses when it weakens. If the euro were instead to weaken, the firm would have to either see its margins drop, at unchanged prices in foreign-currency terms, or lose sales when the product price is increased to compensate for the weaker euro. The firm's budget forecast can be updated with this rule of thumb, in which case its forecasts will reflect not only transaction exposures but also competitive exposures resulting from dynamic pricing strategies.

The competitive exposures just described are not hypothetical. A large fraction of firms competing internationally (or firms in domestic markets that compete with international firms) cope with very similar issues on an ongoing basis. During the Eurozone

---

[2] Producers that are able to easily pass on changes in the exchange rate to their customers through the product price are said to have a high degree of 'pass-through'. A low pass-through, in contrast, implies higher risk because the firm has limited scope to change the price it charges its customers because of competitive effects. It consequently has to absorb more of the exchange rate risk itself.

crisis in 2010 and 2011, the euro was weak against several of the world's currencies. This offered many firms a lifeline in that they could seek to increase exports world-wide. The *Financial Times* (14 September 2017) reported that a Portuguese cement maker was able to survive by cutting costs and, aided by the weak euro, initiating exports to a number of countries around the globe. As the euro was returning to strength in 2017, however, the same firm was feeling the pinch for the exact same reason, facing a competitive onslaught from firms in China, Turkey, and Egypt. Its fortunes are tightly bound to the strength of the euro relative to the currencies of its main competitors.

The Mystery of the 'Underlying' Currency

It should be said that describing commercial exposures to FX risk is challenging, even in relatively favourable circumstances. One thing that makes them hard to quantify is the puzzling concept of 'the underlying currency'. When the term underlying currency is used it should not be taken for granted that people mean the same thing. The term is related to the idea that the currency used to quote the product price in a particular market is not really the currency in which the price is actually determined. Instead, the currency in which the price is set is thought of as the underlying currency. To take an example, aluminium is a global market where the product is priced in US dollars. A producer of aluminium and refined aluminium products with a large presence in Europe tends to generate a steady stream of euros due to invoicing its customers in that currency. Such a company may believe that its 'real' FX exposure related to its sale of aluminium ingots is to the US dollar.

A simple model of the equivalent situation bears this logic out. In Table 2.1 we have assumed a Norwegian producer. Assume that the company's product currently sells for US$200 in the global market. For its customers in the euro-area the firm simply restates this in euro terms (€175) at the prevailing exchange rate. Being a Norwegian company, the firm makes assumptions about the

Table 2.1   Underlying vs transaction currency

	A Base case	B USD ↑	C EUR ↑	D NOK ↓
Product price (USD)	200	200	200	200
EUR/NOK	9.7	9.7	10.3	10.3
USD/NOK	8.5	9.0	8.5	9.0
EUR/USD (implicit)	1.14	1.08	1.21	1.14
Product price (EUR)	175	186	165	175
Revenue (NOK)	1,700	1,800	1,700	1,800

Norwegian krone versus its two most relevant foreign currencies (USD/NOK and EUR/NOK). It is important to note that for any given set of assumptions regarding these two currencies, there is an implied EUR/USD exchange rate that simply follows (1.14 in the base case). If the US dollar strengthens, as manifested by the higher USD/NOK exchange rate (column B), the product price will be restated given the new EUR/USD that follows (now 1.08). Because the US dollar is stronger, this will generate more euros (€186). The revenue measured in kroner is therefore higher (1,800). In contrast, when the euro increases (column C), there is no positive effect on revenue despite the fact that the company transacts in euros and converts those back to kroner! The explanation is that the dollar is now weaker (1.21) so the US$200 price gets the firm fewer euros to be translated into the home currency. The effect of having fewer euros exactly cancels out the beneficial effect of translating those euros at a higher rate.

Shortcomings of the Bottom-up Method

The existence of dynamic exposures creates a challenge when modelling exposures analytically. In the $Q * P * XR$ formula we would have to specify the link between the exchange rate, on the one hand, and volume and price, on the other hand. It goes almost without saying that this quickly gets very complicated. The firm's pricing strategy, and those of its competitors, need to be factored in, along with a host of other factors determining the likely outcome. Perhaps in some cases relatively robust rules of thumb exist and can be used. But experience shows that in most cases it will remain difficult to pin down exactly how, in quantitative terms, exchange rates feed back on volume and price.

Another problem standing in the way of the bottom-up method is poor quality of data inputs. Headquarters typically ask their business units to come up with forecasts of sales volumes and costs, either as part of the budgeting process or as an independent (usually spreadsheet-based) process. The argument behind reaching out in this way is that business units are closer to the action and know their business best. This is of course true. But in asking several business units what their exposure to a specific currency is, one most likely runs into the issue that their understanding of what an exposure is varies greatly. Some may believe that their exposures are determined by the stream of receivables and payables that they observe. Others are more attuned to the concept of 'underlying exposure' and frame their exposure that way (often very subjectively). Other business units may believe that the functional currency of their subsidiaries matters most, referring to the fact that the subsidiaries first report profits in a certain currency, which is then translated to the business unit level from that currency. As a result of these different takes on what an exposure means, the consistency and general quality of exposure estimates from business areas tend to be low and are therefore potentially misleading.

The sheer complexity of today's international firms, however, is perhaps what really shoots the bottom-up approach down. Take Yara International ASA, a Norway-based chemical firm. Its product portfolio includes a wide range of fertilizers and foliar applications. They have sales in some 160 countries world-wide. Production and main distribution centres are located in 60 different countries, in addition to local outlets, on six continents. Input factors are sourced world-wide. Ammonia is needed to make fertilizers. Producing ammonia, in turn, requires natural gas. The price of natural gas is hugely influenced by oil prices. The fertilizer and foliar products are priced in different currencies, including currencies in developing countries considered exotic due to low market liquidity and local regulations. In some cases, these fertilizers are partial substitutes, but one is priced in euros and another in US dollars. If the price in dollars rises too high, customers may switch over to the euro-based product. And so on. The complexity of modelling all of this analytically is mind-boggling.

The takeaway here is that while forecasting exposures and netting them sounds easy, it can be devilishly hard in practice. In surveys, executives regularly cite 'lack of visibility' of FX exposures and the poor reliability of forecasts as major challenges standing in the way of effective FXRM.

The Statistical Method of Exposure Measurement

An alternative to the analytical bottom-up approach to modelling is to quantify exposures using statistical methods. The promise of this approach is as follows. It allows the firm to do away with the costly process of collecting exposure information from business units, which is likely to be biased and inconsistent anyway. It quantifies an average relationship between the firm's performance and exchange rates without regard to the complexity of the business itself. It can furthermore be used to assess the firm's *sustainable* performance and competitiveness by filtering out the windfalls and noise created by exchange rates and other risk factors outside management's control (more on this in Chapter 10).

The statistical method has been pioneered by Lars Oxelheim and Clas Wihlborg in a series of books and articles on the topic. In these publications, some of which are listed at the end of this chapter, the Macroeconomic Uncertainty Strategy (MUST) is explained in more detail.

How does it work? The basic idea is to use regression analysis to quantify exposures. In the regression model, corporate performance is the dependent variable and exchange rates are independent variables. Such a model explains corporate performance as a function of exchange rates [Eq. (2.4)]. In Eq. (2.4), b_0 is a constant, b_1 is the slope coefficient, and e is the error term. The coefficient b_1 indicates how sensitive performance is to a change in the exchange rate XR_1. It captures an average, linear relationship between corporate performance and the exchange rate in question.

$$\text{Performance} = b_0 + b_1 XR_1 + e \qquad (2.4)$$

If the firm is exposed to more than one currency, all of them can be entered into the model, which then becomes a multivariate regression [Eq. (2.5)]. Multivariate regression is an important tool because it allows us to investigate how sensitive firm performance is to changes in an exchange rate, holding other exchange rates constant. Exchange rates are often correlated (tend to move together), because if the home currency weakens it tends to do so against all other currencies simultaneously (more on this in Chapter 8). So, unless other relevant rates are added to the model, the single coefficient b_1 may capture the combined effect of several correlated variables rather than the marginal impact of the exchange rate itself.

$$\text{Performance} = b_0 + b_1 XR_1 + b_2 XR_2 + \ldots + b_n XR_n + e \qquad (2.5)$$

The exposure model is not limited to exchange rates. It is possible to add other market or macroeconomic variables. Generally, any price, rate, or index which has a potential impact on the firm's performance is of potential interest. Oxelheim and Wihlborg point to two categories of variables that often have important roles for understanding commercial exposure: interest rates and inflation rates. Interest rates influence the general demand in the economy, and are especially important to consider for firms that sell capital-intense goods where customers rely on credit for their purchase. Including inflation rates in the model means that the coefficients on exchange rates need to be interpreted a bit differently. They now capture the firm's exposure to changes in the real, as opposed to nominal, exchange rates. In principle, competitive effects are determined by real exchange rates. If the change in the nominal exchange rate merely reflects different inflation rates in the two countries concerned, competitiveness may in fact be largely unaffected.

Equation (2.6) incorporates interest rates (IR) and inflation rates (IF) in addition to exchange rates. XR, IR, and IF in Eq. (2.6) should not be understood as necessarily a single variable. IR, for example, represents an arbitrary number of interest rates to which the firm has commercial exposure (depending on which geographical markets it operates in).

$$\text{Performance} = b_0 + b_1 XR_1 + b_2 IR_2 + b_3 IF_3 + e \qquad (2.6)$$

Which variables should be considered in a statistical exposure model? The list of variables that go into the analysis should come from a fundamental analysis of the firm's industry, business model, and competitive dynamics, as indicated by Box 2.1. The final model will contain a subset of variables from the list of candidates revealed by this analysis. A mix of economic and statistical analysis determines which variables are ultimately included. The exposure model should make sense based on the fundamental analysis, but also have good statistical properties like explanatory power, normally distributed error terms, and statistical significance.

In the statistical method, corporate performance can be measured at different levels. Normally one tries to quantify the exposure model so that it captures commercial exposure as cleanly as possible. Net income is usually too influenced by financial and temporary effects to be a good measure of commercial performance. Income before interest and taxes (EBIT) is usually a better choice, especially if it has been adjusted for non-core operating effects ($EBIT_{Adj}$). Breaking down $EBIT_{Adj}$ into different operating segments can also help estimate models with good properties.

Other implementation issues include the choice of time resolution and length of time period for estimating the model. In most cases, the analysis is done on quarterly data. This is the rhythm that both the internal and external reporting processes follow in most firms. Using annual data would lead to too few observations being available to estimate the model. The further back in time we go, the more data points become available, which improves the estimation. However, data becomes less informative the further removed it is from the present. Firms reinvent themselves at sometimes astonishing rates through acquisitions and divestments, to the point where data points beyond a few years do not count for much since the firm looked very different then. As a general rule of thumb though, at least 20 quarters should be included in the model, but more if the firm hasn't undergone any major transformations. If there have been structural changes, the strategy of breaking down performance into smaller operating segments can offer a way to quantify the exposure model in a reliable way.

How the exposure model is to be interpreted depends on whether the data has been transformed before the model is estimated. When the original, untransformed variables are used, the model is said to be in 'levels'. Regression models work best, however, if the series used do not drift, or trend, over time, which exchange rates (and corporate performance) are known to do. It is therefore safer to estimate the model after the variables have been 'de-trended' by calculating the change, or percentage change. These transformations produce series with a more stable average value, which are therefore better suited for regression analysis. Equation (2.7) shows a hypothetical exposure model for a producing firm based in England. The model has been estimated on quarterly data using variables expressed as percentage changes.

$$\%\Delta EBIT_{Adj} = 0.01 + 0.6 * \%\Delta \frac{USD}{GBP}$$
$$- 0.25 * \%\Delta \frac{EUR}{GBP} - 0.1 * \%\Delta WTI \qquad (2.7)$$

How should we interpret the model in Eq. (2.7)? First of all, it informs us about the average percentage change in $EBIT_{Adj}$ to percentage changes in the three independent variables: the USD/GBP and EUR/GBP exchange rates, and the oil price (WTI, Western Texas Intermediate). The model indicates that as the dollar becomes stronger there is a positive effect on performance. For a 10% increase in USD/GBP, the average effect on $EBIT_{Adj}$ is a 6% increase (this sensitivity is derived holding EUR/GBP and WTI constant). Most likely, this firm's main export market is the USA, generating a revenue stream in US dollars that creates a positive relation. Competitive effects are also possible. Since the firm's cost base is in sterling, a stronger dollar means that the firm benefits from a stronger dollar vis-à-vis its US competitors (whose cost base is largely in dollars). The impact of a stronger euro, however, is negative. If the euro appreciates by 10% there is an average decrease in quarterly $EBIT_{Adj}$ of 2.5%. This could come about if the firm is sourcing its input factors partly from the euro-area. Similarly, an increase in the oil price leads to a negative effect on performance, presumably because it generates higher energy costs.

A statistical exposure model is a cost-efficient way to generate exposure coefficients since it does not rely on a data collection process involving business units. It is also indifferent to the scale of the firm's business operations: average effects are quantified just as well when the firm is large and complex. In fact, the case for a statistical exposure model is even stronger in these cases. The average influence of exchange rates on pricing strategies, and on the general demand for the firm's products, gets factored into the estimates. Any natural hedges that exist throughout the business are also automatically taken into account. That is, the coefficients in the model indicate the firm's net exposure to each exchange rate.

The statistical approach to exposure measurement thus offers a viable alternative for many firms that are frustrated by cumbersome and heavy data collecting processes related to bottom-up forecasts of commercial exposures. Rather than getting inconsistent, poor-quality estimates of exposures from such processes, the exposure model informs management about how corporate performance, on a net basis, responds to changes in exchange rates.

Key Chapter Takeaways

➢ Commercial exposure refers to how the firm's core operating cash flow responds to changes in exchange rates.
➢ An important shift in FXRM is moving away from managing exposures on near-term transactions to managing exposures on aggregated net cash flows on a firm-wide basis.

➢ Firms often struggle with poor data quality and inconsistent methodologies when attempting to forecast commercial exposures, which is a major challenge in FXRM.

➢ Due to the vast complexity of today's multinational firms, quantifying a firm's commercial exposure with a 'bottom-up' approach (i.e. building up cash flow forecasts from forecasted unit sales) is often exceedingly difficult.

➢ A statistical exposure model offers an alternative approach, in which a neutral, average relationship between operating performance and exchange rates is quantified using regression analysis.

➢ The statistical exposure model approach allows the firm to avoid the complicated data collection process and inconsistencies associated with the bottom-up method, and thus offers an economical alternative to quantifying commercial exposures.

Further Reading

Andrén, N., H. Jankensgård, and L. Oxelheim. 2005. Exposure-based cash-flow-at-risk: An alternative to value-at-risk for industrial companies. *Journal of Applied Corporate Finance* **17**, 76–86.

Oxelheim, L. and C. Wihlborg. 2008. *Corporate Decision-making with Macroeconomic Uncertainty*. New York: Oxford University Press.

Chapter 3
Net Income
Exposure to FX

I n most of the preceding chapter we took the view of an exporting firm with its cost base in its home currency. This structure gives the most straightforward of FX exposures: foreign-denominated cash flows that need to be converted to home currency. As firms grow and become larger, however, the issue of international expansion tends to come up on the agenda at some point. This can be achieved by setting up selling and/or production units in another country. It can also be done through acquisitions. Perhaps acquiring the foreign firm is considered a more efficient way to expand compared to gradually building up a presence in that market through organic expansion.

Regardless of the form it takes, the creation of foreign subsidiaries leads to the next step in FX exposure management. We are now talking about a consolidated group with at least one foreign subsidiary, which changes the rules of the game quite substantially. Why? Because foreign subsidiaries are legal entities often denominated in a currency different from the one the firm uses to prepare its consolidated accounts. This gives rise to translation effects, as the exchange rates needed to translate the subsidiaries' accounts into home currency fluctuate between different balance sheet dates.

There may also be translation effects on assets and liabilities that the parent company holds in its own books, for example, if it issues debt in foreign currency.

Firms often take these translation effects seriously, especially when they have to be reported in net income. A firm's net income is therefore exposed to FX in more ways than through the commercial exposure discussed in the previous chapter. Corporate performance is indeed multifaceted: firms simultaneously have to manage several performance measures that they care about, and it would be naïve to think that we can maintain a narrow focus on commercial exposures.

A major theme in this book is that firms, in their quest to manage these multiple performance indicators, often face trade-offs: the instruments used to manage a cash flow exposure often have unintended effects on net income because they have to be either translated or fair valued. In this chapter we tackle these issues straight on. We look at how the need to translate certain assets and liabilities leads to potentially more, not less, volatility in net income, despite the fact that in many cases they do achieve a more balanced net exposure from a cash flow perspective. A solid grasp of the mechanisms behind them is essential to be an effective FX risk manager.

A few notes on terminology before we continue. We will refer to 'gains or losses' as GLs to preserve space. For the same reason, we may abbreviate 'assets and liabilities' as ALs. 'FXGLs' are gains and losses reported in net income related to the translation of asset and liabilities in foreign currency. The asset 'plant, property, and equipment' will be written as PPE for short.

The Basics of Translation Exposure

At each balance sheet date, the firm converts (translates) all its assets and liabilities into the functional currency of the parent company. In most cases, this is done using what is referred to as the 'current rate method', meaning that it is the end-of-period exchange rates that are to be used. An alternative method exists, called the 'temporal method', which uses the historical exchange rate from the point in time when the asset or liability was created. Obviously, there will be less volatility in the financial statements when the historical rather than the current rate is used. But it will also be less realistic. After all, shifts in exchange rates do affect the economic value of the investments the firm has made and the liabilities it has incurred. Therefore, the temporal method is rarely used.

In the current rate method, all assets and liabilities are translated using the closing rates in each reporting period. The firm's equity is not actually translated. The lines that appear under this section – share capital, additional paid-in capital, retained earnings, and so on – continue to be reported at their historical values. Instead, specific lines in equity that exist only for this purpose *adjust* to the translation effects that occur when assets and liabilities are converted into the parent company's functional currency.

Unlike assets and liabilities, the income generated by subsidiaries with a different functional currency than the parent is not converted using end-of-period exchange rates. Instead, the average exchange rates during the period are used, which is normally calculated as the average of all realized daily exchange rates in the period. The logic behind this is that the income is supposed to have been created at an even pace throughout the period. Translating an income generated during an entire quarter with the closing rate would misrepresent the firm's actual performance. Therefore, the average is preferred.[1]

Translating assets and liabilities using the closing rates creates FXGLs. An asset denominated in foreign currency, for example, will be worth less measured in terms of the home currency if the foreign currency weakens. A lower asset value implies a loss. Similarly, a gain will be produced if a liability is denominated in foreign currency and the foreign currency weakens. The logic is that it will take fewer units of home currency to service that liability

---

[1] Some companies, however, operate systems that monitor the exchange rate obtained in each business transaction and can therefore create a more precise estimate by matching each transaction during the quarter with the relevant exchange rate. There is then no need to use the average rate as a simplification.

Table 3.1   Translation of debt into US dollars (US company perspective)

	Mar 30	Jun 30
EUR/USD	1.15	1.20
Balance sheet		
Debt (€/mn)	200	200
Debt ($/mn)	230	240
Net income		
Unrealized FX loss ($/mn)		(10) (= 230 − 240)

than previously thought. Table 3.1 shows the basic computation of a GL on a euro-denominated debt liability, from the perspective of a US company, when there is a change in the exchange rate. To keep it simple, the example assumes no instalments on the loan, and ignores the interest payments related to it. In Table 3.1, the stronger euro means that the euro-denominated liability becomes more expensive for a firm based in the USA. This FX-driven difference between the value of the liability on two different balance sheet dates creates a loss the firm has to report in net income.

FXGLs are either realized or unrealized. Unrealized GLs are pure revaluation effects that have no impact on cash flow. GLs become realized when the contract underpinning the asset or liability is cash-settled at maturity. The total FXGL, which is reported in the net income statement, is the sum of these two components. Note that unrealized vs realized GLs is not a distinction made in accounting standards, nor are they supposed to be disclosed separately on a gross basis, as in the example. Only the net is normally reported externally. For analytical purposes (i.e. in forecasts of financial statements in a spreadsheet application) it makes sense to include and keep track of both. Doing so makes calculating the total net GL easier, and they also have different implications for the cash balance.

Table 3.2 illustrates how an unrealized GL ultimately becomes a realized one at maturity. The example assumes that the debt contract, initiated on 30 March, is due for repayment on 30 December, so that the GL becomes realized in the fourth quarter.

Table 3.2   Unrealized vs realized gains and losses (US company balance sheet)

	Mar 30	Jun 30	Sep 30	Dec 30
EUR/USD	1.15	1.20	1.25	1.22
Balance sheet				
Debt (€/mn)	200	200	200	
Debt ($/mn)	230	240	250	—
Cash flow statement ($/mn)				
Proceeds from borrowing	230	—	—	—
Repayment of loan	—	—	—	(244)
Net income statement ($/mn)				
Unrealized FXGL	—	(10)	(10)	20
Realized FXGL ($/mn)	—	—	—	(14) (= 230 − 244)
Total FXGL ($/mn)	—	(10)	(10)	6

The key to understanding the example is that, at settlement, all the previously *accumulated* unrealized GLs are reversed. At 30 September the accumulated unrealized loss is US$20mn, which is subsequently reversed (with a positive sign). At 30 December the loss becomes realized (calculated as the value of debt at maturity less the original value, US$244mn minus US$230mn). In the fourth quarter, the firm reports the sum of the reversed unrealized loss and the realized one in the income statement. In the example, the exchange rate improves slightly in the fourth quarter, which has the consequence that the firm reverses a larger loss than the actual realized loss. Perhaps counter-intuitively, the firm therefore shows a total FX gain in this quarter. This merely follows from the fact that the firm has booked, and reported, larger losses in the past than what actually turned out to happen. Reported FXGLs must always be understood in the context of previously reported (accumulated) GLs on the contract in question.

Monetary vs Non-monetary Assets

An important thing to keep in mind is that, from a net income perspective, only the translation effects on monetary assets and liabilities count. Gains and losses on non-monetary items, in contrast, are reported in other comprehensive income (to be covered in the next chapter). The difference between what constitutes a monetary vs a non-monetary item is therefore of interest. The key to understanding the difference is that monetary assets and liabilities have a fixed value measured in units of currency. A loan, for example, is a contractual obligation where the nominal amount to be repaid is stated in a specific currency (e.g. US dollars). This is different compared to PPE, for example. PPE are assets that the firm has invested in because they are needed to sustain business operations. In a profitable firm, these assets yield cash flows, which in turn form the basis for the firm's value. But there is no fixed number of currency units to be paid or received related to the PPE itself, and hence it is a non-monetary asset. Table 3.3 lists some common ALs for both categories.

To understand a firm's total FXGL relating to a particular currency, one must begin by adding up all the monetary ALs in that currency in all the legal entities belonging to the firm. The net monetary translation exposure is found by subtracting liabilities from assets. The resulting net exposure can be either positive or negative. If the number is positive, the firm has more assets than liabilities and will gain if the foreign currency strengthens. If negative, the liabilities exceed the assets, and the firm stands to gain if the foreign currency weakens. Table 3.4 contains a simple balance sheet where the functional currency of the parent is US dollars (*note*: the assumptions in Table 3.4 are not related to Table 3.1 or 3.2!). We

Table 3.3   Monetary vs non-monetary assets and liabilities

Monetary	Non-monetary
Cash	Plant, property, and equipment
Debt	Goodwill
Trade receivables	Inventory
Trade payables	Intangible assets
Current tax liability	Investment in associates
(And others)	(And others)

Table 3.4   Monetary vs non-monetary items in home currency (US company balance sheet)

Assets ($/mn)		Liabilities and equity ($/mn)	
Cash (M)	10	Current debt (M)	87
Trade receivables (M)	12	Trade payables (M)	8
Inventory (NM)	45	Non-current debt (M)	92
PPE (NM)	226	Pension liability (NM)	36
Long-term receivables (M)	77	Share capital	100
Intangible assets (NM)	80	Retained earnings	127
Total assets	*450*	*Total liabilities and equity*	*450*

first do a line-by-line classification into either monetary (M) or non-monetary (NM) assets and liabilities. Again, note that equity items in subsidiaries (share capital and retained earnings in the example) are not actually translated, so we need not classify them.

The next step is to produce a statement showing the net amounts for all the ALs that have been classified as monetary. This is to be done *for each currency* that the firm has an exposure to. Table 3.5 continues the example and shows how all the monetary items can be expressed in foreign currency terms (euros in this case). Note that these amounts in Table 3.5 do not add up to the total balance sheet number shown in Table 3.4. Assume that the EUR/USD exchange rate at the time of our analysis is 1.20. Then we can see that 21 * 1.20 = US$25.2 mn for non-current debt does not equate to the amount appearing in the consolidated balance sheet, which is US$87 mn. This happens because the firm does not have short-term debt only in euros. The remainder (87 − 25.2) is made up of loans in other currencies.

Summing all the euro-denominated monetary assets in Table 3.5 and subtracting the corresponding liabilities gives us a net liability of €28 mn. This number informs us of the translation GL that would result if the EUR/USD were to change. If the change compared to the previous quarter is from 1.15 to 1.20, we know that the revaluation will cause a loss of US$1.4 mn [(1.20 − 1.15) * €28 mn]. It must be a loss because the euro is now stronger (it takes 1.2 dollars rather

Table 3.5   Monetary assets and liabilities in euros (US parent company perspective)

Assets (€/mn)		Liabilities (€/mn)	
Cash	4	Current debt	21
Trade receivables	8	Trade payables	3
Inventory	—	Non-current debt	80
PPE	—	Pension liability	—
Long-term receivables	64	Share capital	—
Intangible assets	—	Retained earnings	—
Monetary assets	*76*	*Monetary liabilities*	*104*
Net EUR monetary position = 76 – 104 = (28)			

than 1.15 to buy one euro) and the firm has more liabilities than assets in euros. The combination of a stronger foreign currency and a net monetary liability in that currency leads to a loss that must be reported in the net income statement.

The Issue of Functional vs Transaction Currency

The previous section presents a somewhat simplified picture of how translation GLs affect net income. It is not actually the case that *all* monetary ALs in foreign currency give rise to an exposure. There are circumstances that create exceptions to the basic rule. To understand why, we need to make a brief detour and discuss the issue of functional vs transaction currency. Functional currency has been covered already, but we need to define transaction currency. By transaction currency we mean the currency in which a monetary AL is denominated.

The reason why things get a bit more complicated is that most firms are actually corporate groups, that is to say a collection of different legal entities tied together through ownership. One of these legal entities will be the parent company, which holds controlling stakes in the others, referred to as subsidiaries. When we speak of 'the firm', we usually mean the consolidated corporate group, consisting of the assets and liabilities held by its various entities.

The fact that there are multiple legal units in a corporate group is an important observation from the point of view of understanding FXGLs. It means that a specific asset or liability in principle can be held by any entity in the group, and the different entities *need not have the same functional currency*. In fact, it is quite unlikely that all entities have the same functional currency. As discussed previously, as a firm becomes larger it tends to start establishing or acquiring other firms, often internationally, which are then consolidated into the corporate group. The result is that most firms above a certain size are multinational firms with a potentially significant number of foreign subsidiaries. And because they continue to be separate legal entities, the units still need to prepare financial statements in their respective functional currency.

Why does the fact that the parent company and subsidiaries can have different functional currencies matter to FXRM? The answer is that an FXGL can only occur if the currency of the monetary asset or liability is different from the functional currency of the legal entity in which it is held. An FXGL can occur at the parent level, but also at the subsidiary level if the subsidiary has a mismatch between its functional currency and its net monetary AL. FXGLs occurring at the subsidiary level are then reported in the *consolidated* net income, translated at the prevailing exchange rate.

An example will clarify this. In Tables 3.1 and 3.2 the debt was in euros, held by a US firm. Implicitly, we assumed that the loan had been taken up by the US parent. A euro loan in a US company obviously creates an exposure to the EUR/USD. But what if the loan had instead been taken by a subsidiary based in the euro-area, say in Germany? From the viewpoint of this subsidiary, there would be no exposure. To them, the euro loan cannot be translated because it is already in the same currency as the functional currency. The subsidiary would therefore not report any FXGL, regardless of how much the exchange rate moves. The way accounting standards work, if there is no FXGL in the subsidiary that formally owns the asset or liability, it cannot be recognized at the consolidated level either.

The upshot is that not all monetary ALs held by a corporate group give rise to FXGLs. We need to look for cases where the functional currency of the entity is identical to that of the transaction currency in question. Whenever such a combination is found, we need to adjust the calculation of the net monetary position because this item does not represent an exposure in the consolidated accounts. Rather than summing up the various monetary ALs in that currency (as we did in Table 3.5), we must remove the cases where the functional currency and transaction currency are the same. That is, the sensitivity of the firm's net income to translation effects is determined not by its net monetary position but rather by its net *adjusted* monetary position.

The Exposure Matrix

How can we arrive at the adjusted monetary position, which correctly indicates how the firm's net income responds to translation effects? Here it helps to think in terms of a matrix. In this matrix, the functional currency of the entity in question is on the *x*-axis and the transaction currency is on the *y*-axis. The instances where the functional currency and the transaction currency are the same, and therefore not exposed, are found *on the diagonal* in this matrix. This gives the information we need to correctly calculate the net exposure as it applies to consolidated net income.

Let us run the two different possibilities in our simple example (assumptions are based on Table 3.1) through such a currency exposure matrix. The upper matrix (Panel A) in Table 3.6 shows the situation where the US-based parent company takes out the euro loan. The euro–dollar mismatch ensures that the debt is off the diagonal and therefore exposed. The lower matrix (Panel B) shows that the debt ends up on the diagonal when the subsidiary based in Germany takes out the loan. No FXGL will be generated when transaction currency and functional currency are identical, so we need to consider this debt 'unexposed' and therefore exclude

Table 3.6   Exposure matrix with external debt in foreign currency

Panel A: Euro debt held by US parent			
		Functional currency	
Transaction currency		EUR	USD
	EUR		(200)
	USD		
Panel B: Euro debt held by German subsidiary			
		Functional currency	
Transaction currency		EUR	USD
	EUR	(200)	
	USD		

it when summing up the monetary ALs that determine the firm's net income exposure to that currency.

Examples of exposure matrices can be varied endlessly. The basic takeaway is that sorting firms' balance sheets into monetary vs non-monetary ALs is not quite enough to understand how net income is exposed. We need to do a second review where each monetary AL is checked for both transactional and functional currency and adjust the calculation whenever they coincide.

Let us look at a more comprehensive example of net income exposure using the matrix approach. Assume we know the following (important: numbers are now based on Table 3.5 instead of Table 3.1!). The cash in euros is held entirely by a euro-based subsidiary, as are half of the trade receivables and all of the trade payables. The current debt is held entirely by the parent company, as is the non-current debt. The long-term receivable is a euro loan that the parent company has issued to another operating company outside the group with which it has a long-term relationship.

What would the exposure matrix look like in this case? Table 3.7 illustrates what happens. Any positions that are due to transactions in the subsidiary end up on the diagonal. Only euro transactions in the US parent now contribute to the firm's net exposure. The net *adjusted* monetary position is a different number than the net

Table 3.7   Exposure matrix with assets and liabilities of both parent and subsidiary

Transaction currency		Functional currency	
		EUR	USD
	EUR	5	*(33)*
	USD		
US parent net EUR position is calculated as: 4 + 64 − 80 − 21 = (33)			
German subsidiary net EUR position is calculated as: 4 + 4 − 3 = 5			
Net adjusted EUR monetary position = (33)			

monetary position calculated in Table 3.5 (−€33 mn vs −€28 mn). The reason is that in the original calculation in Table 3.5 we did not take into account the functional currency of the entity in which the AL was actually held. Applying the exposure matrix leads to a new number that will better correspond to the GLs the firm actually experiences in its net income as a result of fluctuations in the EUR/USD exchange rate. The sum of the monetary positions in euros, however, will be the same as in Table 3.5 (−33 + 5 = −€28 mn).

External Exposures on Internal Transactions

It takes some getting used to the fact that not all monetary items are exposed due to functional currency considerations. But one quickly comes around to the idea. At the end of the day, a legal entity has to produce its financial statements, and only when that is done is there something that can be consolidated into the corporate group's net income. If no gain or loss occurs on the subsidiary level, there is nothing to consolidate further up in the system. But an extension of the same principle carries a consequence that is perhaps more difficult to accept, because it seems to run counter to common sense. We are talking about the fact that internal transactions (i.e. transactions between two legal entities that are part of the same corporate group) can lead to GLs that have to be reported in the consolidated net income.

This is contrary to how we expect things to be. We normally assume that all internal transactions, and everything connected to them, disappear upon preparing the consolidated accounts. If Unit A owes Unit B 10 mn, it does not really matter if both are fully owned subsidiaries in the same group. It should not matter if money is kept in the left or right pocket. And disappear they indeed do, as long as we are talking about internal assets and liabilities. The receivable owned by Unit B is eliminated against the payable of Unit A, so on a group level the net is zero. Things do not always cancel each other out so neatly, however, when it comes to FXGLs related to these internal transactions. The story is essentially the same as before. It happens because the transaction currency coincides with the functional currency of one subsidiary but not that of the other (or that of the parent).

So far, we have assumed that the loan has been taken out by either the parent or the subsidiary. A third option is that the parent borrows the money and then uses those funds to extend a loan to its subsidiary. Such internal loans will, strange as it may seem, change the net adjusted monetary position of the group. Table 3.8 illustrates what happens if the parent company lends its subsidiary €40 mn out of the €80 mn it borrowed long term (Table 3.8 is based on the assumptions in Table 3.5, where the non-current debt is €80 mn). The loan creates a liability that must be subtracted from the subsidiary's position in euros, creating a negative net amount. But since this position appears on the diagonal, it has no impact on the net income exposure of the consolidated group. The parent, for its part, adds a €40 mn debt receivable to its position in euros (the claim on its subsidiary), which jumps from −33 to 7. So, the company has, through an internal loan, magically reversed the sign of its net adjusted monetary position in euros! The internal loan will, simply because different group entities have different functional currencies, create FXGLs that must be reported in the consolidated financial statements.

Table 3.8   Exposure matrix with internal and external transactions

Transaction currency		Functional currency	
		EUR	USD
	EUR	−35	7
	USD		
US parent net EUR position is calculated as: 4 + 64 − 80 − 21 + 40 = 7			
German subsidiary net EUR position is calculated as: 4 + 4 − 3 − 40 = −35			
Net adjusted EUR monetary position = 7			

Table 3.9 shows how this happens. It singles out the internal transaction and how it is accounted for in both the parent and the subsidiary. In the parent, because of the mismatch between transaction and functional currency, there is indeed an FXGL when the exchange rate moves and the receivable is booked at a higher

Table 3.9   Net income effects with internal and external transactions

	Mar 30	Jun 30
EUR/USD	1.15	1.20
Parent company (functional currency = US dollar)		
Balance sheet		
Internal receivable (€/mn)	40	40
Internal receivable ($/mn)	46	48
Net income ($/mn)		
Unrealized FX gain	0	2 (= 48 − 46)
Subsidiary (functional currency = euro)		
Balance sheet (€/mn)		
Internal payable	40	40
Net income (€/mn)		
Unrealized FXGL	0	0
Consolidated group (functional currency = US dollar)		
Net income ($/mn)		
Unrealized FXGL in parent	0	2
Unrealized FXGL in subsidiary	0	0
Total unrealized FXGL	0	2

EUR/USD (meaning a weaker dollar). We would expect there to be an offsetting loss in the subsidiary so that the gain and loss cancel each other out, just as with the corresponding asset and liability. This fails to happen, however, because the payable in the subsidiary is insensitive to EUR/USD. It has this liability in its own functional currency, so there is no impact.

Key Chapter Takeaways

➢ Aside from commercial exposures to FX, a firm's net income is impacted by translation effects that are to be reported in its financial expenses.

➢ Net income is affected by the translation of monetary assets and liabilities, which are items in the balance sheet with a fixed value measured in units of currency (e.g. debt, receivables, and cash).

➢ When a foreign currency appreciates, monetary assets in that currency produce gains measured in the home currency, whereas monetary liabilities produce losses.

➢ However, translation gains and losses on monetary items are only reported in consolidated net income if there is a mismatch between the functional currency of the legal unit holding it and the transaction currency.

➢ This necessitates an approach involving an exposure matrix in which the transaction currency and the functional currency are mapped out.

➢ Items on the diagonal in the exposure matrix (where transaction currency = functional currency) are not exposed from a consolidated net income point of view.

➢ Contrary to intuition, even internal transactions can give rise to gains and losses in consolidated net income when the two group companies involved have different functional currencies.

Further Reading

Hagelin. N. 2003. Why firms hedge with currency derivatives: An examination of transaction and translation exposure. *Applied Financial Economics* **13**, 55–69.

Jankensgård, H., A. Alviniussen, and L. Oxelheim. 2016. Why FX risk management is broken – and what boards need to know to fix it. *Journal of Applied Corporate Finance* **28**, 46–61.

Chapter 4
Balance Sheet Exposure to FX

Net income, the focus of the previous chapter, is perhaps the most widely communicated performance metric of them all. It is not surprising that managers try to limit the impact of various external factors, such as exchange rates, on this bottom line. Accounting standards, however, have it such that only some translation GLs are to be reported in net income, namely those relating to monetary ALs. But this does not mean that the translation GLs excluded from net income – relating to non-monetary ALs – are of no importance. They have the potential to affect shareholders' equity and any financial ratio based on it in a major way. This chapter is about mapping out and better understanding these effects.

A real-world episode can illustrate how the translation of non-monetary ALs can take the company's leadership by surprise. The executives and directors of the company in question were pleased to announce the firm's largest profits ever. Much to their surprise, however, equity did not increase in that year despite profits running in the billions. The explanation was a translation loss on non-monetary assets that cancelled out the positive effect that net income had on equity. Management had not anticipated this, nor could they easily see how it came about. The mechanisms were poorly understood.

Sometimes this kind of translation GL can have real consequences. As discussed in Chapter 1, a case can be made for avoiding financial ratios reaching critical threshold levels specified in loan covenants. A deteriorating equity ratio, for example, could trigger covenants in a loan agreement that limits management's ability to run the firm optimally. A credit rating may in some circumstances also hinge critically on financial ratios not breaching critical thresholds by too much, or for too long. Translation effects on shareholders' equity can often be quite large, and therefore hold the potential to dislocate key financial ratios substantially.

Avoiding surprises and safeguarding financial ratios present two arguments as to why managing these translation effects should be part of a programme for FXRM. But maybe it was incorrect to think of them as merely 'paper effects' in the first place. In most cases, translation GLs on non-monetary assets refer to the net assets (equity) in foreign subsidiaries. Take a company that owns a subsidiary denominated in a foreign currency. If that currency weakens, the home currency value of the investment in the subsidiary will be lower not just in the world of accounting, but also from an economic perspective. This is because the expected future cash flows from that entity will also be reduced, in home currency terms, from the depreciation of the foreign currency. While this may not be a first-order concern to managers, it is worth keeping in mind that there is an economic foundation for the translation GLs.

The Basics of Non-monetary Assets and Liabilities

Non-monetary assets and liabilities are ALs with no fixed amount of currency to be paid (or received) in a highly likely transaction. Rather, they are assets purchased, and liabilities incurred, in the process of building cash-flow-generating business operations.

To the extent they are held by foreign subsidiaries, these non-monetary ALs have to be translated into the functional currency of the parent company. In this context, one often hears about 'translating the equity of subsidiaries'. It is actually more correct to speak of translating the assets and liabilities of subsidiaries. While equity of course is the difference between assets and liabilities, it is an important principle that the translation is not of equity per se. Instead, equity adjusts in different ways when ALs are translated.

There are two basic ways that equity in the consolidated financial statements responds to the translation of assets and liabilities in foreign subsidiaries. One is through the equity account retained earnings. Translation gains add to retained earnings, whereas losses subtract from them. The channel through which this happens is net income. But, as discussed in the previous chapter, net income only records the effects from monetary items. Therefore, we need another equity account to deal with the translation GLs of non-monetary ALs. This account is called the translation reserve and is part of other reserves. But actually, that is not all of it. We also need another income statement to connect these translation GLs and shareholders' equity, because we cannot use net income for this purpose. This brings us to the statement of other comprehensive income (OCI), which is where these GLs are shown. In most financial reports, this statement is reported just below the net income statement. The relationship between translation GLs and shareholders' equity can be summarized as in Figure 4.1.

A firm's income thus comes in two varieties: net income and other comprehensive income. These two elements sum up to total income, which in the accounting standards is referred to as 'comprehensive income':

Comprehensive income = Net income + Other comprehensive income

Other comprehensive income is an interesting device. While in principle it is supposed to inform about the totality of the firm's gains and losses in a year, thus complementing net income, it often comes across more like a mechanism needed to reconcile the in- and outgoing balance sheet given various rules concerning the accounting of assets and liabilities. It contains a set of unrealized GLs that, according to accounting standards, are not supposed

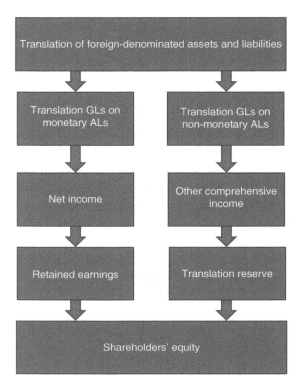

Figure 4.1   Translation effect and shareholders' equity

to be included in net income. It is as if the standard-setters have sought to protect net income from the excessive volatility that would result from including these unrealized GLs. But they are still gains and losses, so at the end of the day they need to have an impact on equity. This is where OCI comes into the picture: it is the income statement where the effects of various quirkier accounting principles tend to end up, such as those relating to pension plans and, of course, translation of non-monetary ALs.

Interestingly, people with an accounting background will sometimes insist that OCI is not an income statement per se. It is simply the place where gains and losses that are 'charged directly to equity' are reported. That is, they do not view OCI as the mechanism whereby these GLs find their way into equity. Rather, the gains and losses hit equity directly, and are then shown, or compiled, in OCI. In this view, OCI is not an intermediate step, or channel, but instead a summary of the items that have been charged to equity. Obviously, this is a matter of semantics. From an analytical point of view it makes more sense to think of them as two different kinds of income statements that together add up to total (comprehensive) income, to which all changes in the value of assets or liabilities ultimately must be related.

Our focus is on understanding how translation GLs travel through the firm's financial statements. To reduce heavy terminology, we will label translation GLs that appear in net income as 'FXGL' and those in comprehensive income as 'CTGL', where CT stands for 'currency translation' (in financial reports, CTGL is often referred to as 'translation difference').

$$\text{Total translation GL} = \text{FXGL} + \text{CTGL}$$

Table 4.1 illustrates the basics of translation exposures. The example concerns a US parent company which issues equity and uses those funds to invest in PPE through an England-based subsidiary. The translation exposure arises from having to convert the subsidiary's assets and liabilities back to US dollars. Initially the GBP/USD exchange rate is 1.40 but changes to 1.50 in the following period. Because PPE is the only asset that needs to be translated, the net AL position is £100 mn. The net AL position in a currency is the difference between all assets and liabilities in that currency (regardless of their status as monetary or non-monetary).

The net AL position dictates what the change in shareholders' equity from translation *ultimately has to be* when the relevant exchange rate moves (GBP/USD in this case). That is how we can think about this number. But it does not inform us about exactly *how* this change plays out in terms of whether these translation GLs affect net income or not. The parent is assumed to be wholly equity-financed, so there are no monetary ALs in the example. As the exchange rate goes to 1.50 at the end of June the PPE is

Table 4.1 Translation of non-monetary assets

	Mar 30	June 30
	GBP/USD = 1.40	GBP/USD = 1.50
Subsidiary (functional currency = pound sterling; numbers in £/mn)		
PPE	100	100
Share capital	100	100
Parent company (functional currency = US dollar; numbers in US$/mn)		
Shares in subsidiary	140	140
Share capital	140	140
Translation exposure to pound sterling		
Net AL position:	100	(PPE in subsidiary)
Net monetary position:	—	(no pound-denominated debt)
Consolidated financial statements (functional currency = US dollar; numbers in US$/mn)		
Net income		
FXGL	0	0
Other comprehensive income		
CTGL	0	10
Balance sheet		
PPE	140	150
Share capital	140	140
Translation reserve	0	10

translated at 1.50 * 100 = US$150 mn, which is US$10 mn more than in the previous period. Because the gain is related to a non-monetary asset (PPE), it bypasses net income and instead is shown as a CTGL in other comprehensive income. Importantly, share capital (and retained earnings) in the parent company remain unaffected. Instead, to balance the balance sheet the CTGL ends up in the translation reserve, which is an equity account that exists solely for the purpose of 'storing' accumulated translation GLs. We are able to confirm that the total change in equity after the exchange rate change, US$10 mn, is indeed that implied by the net AL position, which can be verified as $(1.50 - 1.40) * 100 = US\$10$ mn.

Reconciling the Exposure Matrix with Shareholders' Equity

At this point we need to revisit an issue raised in the previous chapter, namely that monetary ALs are not exposed from a net income perspective if the transaction currency coincides with the functional currency of the entity that holds it. What happens, to give the short version, is that the gains and losses related to these 'unexposed' monetary ALs move into CTGL. This is what is required to balance the books. Otherwise, these GLs would 'go missing' and the translation of foreign assets and liabilities would not match with the total income reported. To learn more about this, we will look at what happens to translation exposures if we introduce a monetary AL where there is a mismatch between the transaction and functional currencies (Table 4.2). We then proceed to analyse the case where no such mismatch occurs (Table 4.3).

In Table 4.2 we have altered the assumptions compared to Table 4.1 in only one way. Instead of being fully equity financed, the parent company has now raised a loan in pounds sterling to finance its investment in the subsidiary. This suggests a £50 mn debt at the original exchange rate. As a result, we need to subtract this debt from the PPE asset to get the new net AL position, which is now $100 - 50 = £50$ mn. The company benefits from a stronger pound because it holds assets in that currency, but there is a partly offsetting loss on its pound-denominated liability. When the exchange rate changes to 1.50, this can be seen as a CTGL of US$10 mn, reflecting the gain on the PPE, and as an FX loss of −£5 mn, caused by the pound-denominated debt. The loan is a monetary liability, so this translation loss has a negative effect on net income. PPE is not a monetary asset, however, so this translation gain is reported in other comprehensive income instead.

It should be noted that the pound debt is positioned *off the diagonal* in the exposure matrix of this company, which happens because the debt was taken up by the US parent, creating a mismatch between transaction and functional currency. As a result

Table 4.2 Translation effects when functional currency is not equal to transaction currency

	Mar 30	Jun 30
	GBP/USD = 1.40	GBP/USD = 1.50
Subsidiary (functional currency = pound sterling; numbers in £/mn)		
PPE	100	100
Share capital	100	100
Parent company (functional currency = US dollar; numbers in US$/mn)		
Shares in subsidiary	140	140
Debt	70	75
Share capital	70	70
Retained earnings	0	(5)
Translation exposure to pound sterling		
Net AL position	50	(PPE in subsidiary less external debt)
Net monetary position	(50)	(external debt in pounds)
Consolidated financial statements (functional currency = US dollar; numbers in US$/mn)		
Net income		
FXGL	0	(5)
Other comprehensive income		
CTGL	0	10
Balance sheet		
PPE	140	150
Debt	70	75
Share capital	70	70
Retained earnings	0	(5)
Translation reserve	0	10

of being off the diagonal, translation GLs on the loan impact net income. Rather than assuming that monetary ALs *always* lead to net income effects, we should first verify that the mismatch is actually present by recasting the monetary ALs in the shape of an exposure matrix.

In Table 4.3 we modify the setting in the following way. Instead of the loan being taken out by the parent, this is now done by the

Table 4.3 Translation effects when functional currency is equal to transaction currency

	Mar 30	Jun 30
	GBP/USD = 1.40	GBP/USD = 1.50
Subsidiary (functional currency = pound sterling; numbers in £/mn)		
PPE	100	100
Share capital	50	50
Debt	50	50
Parent company (functional currency = US dollar; numbers in US$/mn)		
Shares in subsidiary	70	70
Share capital	70	70
Translation exposure to pound sterling		
Net AL position	50	(PPE less external debt in subsidiary)
Net adjusted monetary position	—	(pound debt in subsidiary not exposed)
Consolidated financial statements (functional currency = US dollar)		
Net income		
FXGL	0	0
Other comprehensive income		
CTGL	0	5
Balance sheet		
PPE	140	150
Debt	70	75
Share capital	70	70
Retained earnings	0	0
Translation reserve	0	5

UK subsidiary, which is therefore assumed to be financed in equal parts by equity and debt. The £50 mn loan is now *on the diagonal* in the firm's exposure matrix, because the transaction currency coincides with the functional currency of the legal entity holding it (the subsidiary). The net AL position of the company as a whole is still £50 mn, however (the PPE asset less the pound debt). When the exchange rate moves to 1.50, the firm's consolidated net income is unaffected despite the debt. This happens because the subsidiary is not exposed: it has the pound as functional currency so it does not register, as far as a debt denominated in pounds is concerned, any gain or loss from a change in the value of the pound.

As before, the firm books a US$10 mn translation gain on the subsidiary's PPE. However, this gain overstates the total gain that is possible given the net AL position of £50 mn. The US$5 mn translation loss on the debt, which is now more expensive from the US perspective, is what ensures that the right net result obtains. The firm cannot report this loss in the net income, though, because there is no such loss registered in any legal entity that is part of the group (because of the debt being on the diagonal in the exposure matrix). For this reason, in order to balance the books, the CTGL records the net of the two directly (a gain of only US$5 mn instead of US$10 mn). One way to put it is that the CTGL (and the translation reserve) 'absorbs' the GLs on the monetary items that sit on the diagonal in the exposure matrix (i.e. the cases where the functional currency is the same as the transaction currency).

Reconciling Internal Transactions with Shareholder's Equity

A similar story is going on for translation GLs related to internal transactions. Recall that the translation of payables and receivables between group companies can 'magically' create GLs that do not disappear when financial statements are consolidated. From the perspective of the firm's shareholder equity this is an impossibility, however. GLs drive equity, and equity cannot be impacted by internal transactions. There must therefore be something that neutralizes the effect of these internally generated GLs on equity. Again, CTGL comes to the rescue. What essentially happens is that there is a mirroring GL in CTGL *with the opposite sign*, such that it perfectly offsets the GL in net income caused by the internal transaction. As a result, there is no net effect on equity, and the books balance.

Table 4.4 illustrates how the financial statements play out when there is an internal transaction. Neither the parent company nor the subsidiary borrows externally. However, instead of financing its subsidiary solely with equity, the parent decides to lend it £50 mn. This amount shows up as an asset in the form of an internal receivable in the parent company. In the subsidiary a new liability is reported

Table 4.4 Translation of non-monetary assets and internal transactions

	Mar 30	Jun 30
	GBP/USD = 1.40	GBP/USD = 1.50
Subsidiary (functional currency = pound sterling; numbers in £/mn)		
PPE	100	100
Internal payable	50	50
Share capital	50	50
Parent company (functional currency = US dollar; numbers in US$/mn)		
Shares in subsidiary	70	70
Internal receivable	70	75
Share capital	140	140
Retained earnings	0	5
Translation exposure to pound sterling		
Net AL position	100	(PPE in subsidiary)
Net monetary position	—	(no external ALs in pounds sterling)
Net adjusted monetary position	50	(internal receivable)
Consolidated financial statements (functional currency = US dollar)		
Net income		
FXGL	0	5
Other comprehensive income		
CTGL	0	5
Balance sheet		
PPE	140	150
Share capital	140	140
Retained earnings	0	5
Translation reserve	0	5

as an internal payable (debt). This configuration creates some interesting effects on the group's exposure to GBP/USD. Since it is an internal transaction, the firm's net AL position is unaffected by it. The translation GLs on the PPE is the only thing that should cause any effect on the group's equity when GBP/USD changes.

But, contrary to our intuition, the net *adjusted* monetary position does change when the internal transaction is debt rather than equity. This is because of how the internal payable and receivable enter the exposure matrix. We now report a £50 mn asset (the parent's receivable) and a £50 mn liability (the subsidiary's payable) in the matrix. Crucially, though they refer to the same transaction in pounds, they end up in different places on the *x*-axis in the matrix. This happens because the subsidiary has pounds as its functional currency, so its pound debt is placed on the diagonal. The US parent's pound receivable is off the diagonal, however, because of the mismatch between functional and transaction currency, thereby creating the preconditions for FXGLs to be reported in consolidated net income.

In Table 4.4 the pound strengthens from 1.40 to 1.50. The parent's receivable is translated at the new rate and a gain of US$5 mn is recorded in net income, which is not countered by a loss in the subsidiary's accounts. This effect on net income pushes retained earnings up from zero to US$5 mn in the consolidated balance sheet. At the same time, the PPE is retranslated from US$140 to US$150. Now we are looking at a total gain of 5 + 10 = US$15 mn, which is incompatible with the net AL position of £100. Given this net AL position, and given the 0.10 change in the exchange rate, the total gain can really only be US$10 mn. The situation is resolved by inserting a loss of −US$5 mn in the CTGL, whose sole purpose it is to neutralize the effect of equity from the FXGL of US$5 mn that appears in net income. The CTGL thus consists of a translation gain of US$10 mn and a 'reconciliation loss' of −US$5 mn, so that what is shown in the OCI is a gain of US$5 mn. This, together with the US$5 mn gain in net income/retained earnings from the parent company's FXGL, in the end produces the overall gain affecting shareholders' equity of US$10 mn we would expect based on the net AL position. So, all is well, except perhaps for the fact that we have the non-intuitive outcome that a CTGL in other comprehensive income is needed to offset the FXGL appearing in net income.

Before leaving this subject, we may reflect on the fact that, from the viewpoint of the parent firm, the FXGL is real once we start talking about realized rather than unrealized effects (the example only contains an unrealized effect). Let us say that the exchange rate does not change further. When the subsidiary eventually repays the loan, those pounds will in fact be worth more in US dollar terms and the parent company sees an increase in its cash position from the internal transaction. With more dollars sitting in the bank at the parent company, why is the gain not real to the company as a whole when the subsidiary only paid back the same amount in its own currency that it borrowed? It is not going to be concerned by the fact that the value of the pound changed in the meantime, because that is its functional currency. To see what is going on, it is easiest to imagine that the subsidiary must take out a loan with a bank, in pounds, to settle the internal payable when it is due. This loan is a new external liability for the consolidated group also. Crucially, the new pound debt enters the books at the new and higher exchange rate, which pushes the value of liabilities up for the consolidated group compared to the situation prior to the strengthening of the pound. If the parent company had borrowed the money in dollars (its own currency) and converted it to pounds at the old exchange rate in order to lend the money to the subsidiary, the value of that liability would be lower, in dollar terms, in comparison with the new liability incurred by the subsidiary. When the subsidiary repays the internal loan, the parent company converts those pounds into dollars, after which it turns around to pay down its own debt with the bank, which exits the books. Effectively, the firm has replaced a dollar loan, converted to pounds at the lower exchange rate, with a loan in pounds valued at the new and higher rate. Therefore, the increase in cash in the parent firm from the internal transaction is offset by a higher value on the consolidated group's external liabilities, and the net effect on equity is zero.

Reconciling Translation of Income with Shareholder's Equity

So far, we have been discussing translation effects related to balance sheet items. However, every quarter a firm has to translate not only the foreign subsidiaries' balance sheet but also their income statement. To illustrate the principles at work, the income we discuss in this section is purely operating, by which we mean lines like revenue, cost of goods sold, and operating costs. To simplify, there are no ingoing monetary balance sheet items producing any GLs in financial expenses, so operating income will be equal to net income. At this point we recall that the rules have it that the average exchange rate shall be applied to translate lines like revenue and expenses because it gives a more descriptive view of operating performance as seen over a whole quarter.

However, due to how the consolidation process works, translating operating income at the average rate is not the end of the story. The consolidation of the subsidiary is illustrated in Table 4.5. The setting in this table is that a Swedish holding company (with no operating activities of its own) has invested in a German subsidiary. During the quarter the EUR/SEK goes from 10 to 10.5, producing an average of 10.25, so the income of the subsidiary in the second quarter is translated using the average of 10.25.[1]

As part of the consolidation process, the parent company translates the subsidiary's balance sheet. After the second quarter, there are two assets that need to be translated: the PPE and a cash position. The cash in the bank comes from the income generated in the quarter (we simplify by assuming that all transactions are paid in cash rather than on credit, and that there are no taxes; we also simplify in that we assume the firm does not depreciate its PPE). These assets are translated using the closing rate of 10.5. The parent at the same time translates the income statement of the subsidiary.

An inconsistency creeps in here because the income in the subsidiary is $20 * 10.25 = 205$ mn krona when translated at the

---

[1] In actuality, the average would be obtained by looking at all daily rates throughout the period, not just the opening and closing rates.

Table 4.5 Translation effects in consolidated income statement

	Mar 30	Jun 30	
EUR/SEK	10	10.5	(average = 10.25)
Subsidiary (functional currency = euro)			
Balance sheet (€/mn)			
PPE	100	100	
Cash	—	20	
Share capital	100	100	
Retained earnings	—	20	
Net income (€/mn)	—	**20**	
Cash flow statement (€/mn)	—	**20**	
Parent company (functional currency = Swedish krona; numbers in SEK million)			
Balance sheet			
Shares in subsidiary	1,000	1,000	
Share capital	1,000	1,000	
Net income	—	—	
Cash flow statement	—	—	
Consolidated group (functional currency = Swedish krona; numbers in SEK million)			
Balance sheet			
PPE	1,000	1,050	
Cash	—	210	
Share capital	1,000	1,000	
Retained earnings	—	205	
Translation reserve	—	55	
Net income			
Income in subsidiary	—	205	
OCI			
Translation difference	—	55	
Cash flow statement	—	**210**	

average rate. However, the same net income has generated a cash balance in the subsidiary that is translated at 20 * 10.50 = 210 mn. This does not square. Using the net income of 205 mn krona in the consolidation leads to a retained earnings number that fails to make the balance sheet balance (5 mn krona are 'missing'). Therefore, a translation difference is introduced to reconcile the two. It is calculated as the income in the subsidiary * (closing rate − average closing rate). This yields $20 * (10.5 − 10.25) = 5$ mn krona, just what we needed to balance the balance sheet.

The euro is appreciating, so the adjustment is positive. This is because the higher closing rate of 10.5 pulls up the value of the cash position in the subsidiary. A positive translation difference is needed because otherwise the income translated using the average will understate the krona value of the income when seen in relation to the cash position it has actually generated at the consolidated level.[2]

Importantly, the translation does not get added to the income statement itself. Instead, it is booked in OCI/translation reserve. But this still serves to close the gap in the balance sheet since it too increases total shareholders' equity. In Table 4.5, note there is a CTGL from translating the PPE in the subsidiary amounting to 50 mn krona, such that the total CTGL is 55 mn (50 mn in translation gain on the PPE plus 5 mn in translation difference). Note also that the cash flow statement increases by 210 mn krona, which is equal to the value of comprehensive income (meaning net income plus OCI). In this simple model, in which cash sales are assumed, income is the only thing that leads to an outgoing value. Comprehensive income must be 210 mn to equate the value of the cash balance measured in krona. Consequently, the cash flow statement must register a cash flow from operations of exactly this amount in krona to reconcile the balance sheet and net income.

The Currency Translation Reserve: A Summary

The CTGL thus performs four functions designed to make sure that the effect on shareholders' equity is consistent with the

---

[2] The net effect is that the income in the subsidiary, at the end of all this, is effectively translated at the closing rate, and not the average rate. It is just that it is divided into two components: an initial translation of the income using the average and then an additional correction for the exchange rate difference.

overall net AL position and income in foreign currency. First, the translation GL on non-monetary ALs. Second, the translation GL on 'unexposed' monetary ALs (those on the diagonal in the exposure matrix). Third, the neutralization of FXGLs caused by internal transactions. Fourth, the translation difference that occurs at the consolidated level when the subsidiaries' income is translated at average exchange rate but their end-of-period balance sheet at the closing rate.

As noted, at the end of the day, the effect on shareholders' equity from translating ALs in a given currency must obey the firm's net AL position in that currency. The net AL position is simply the difference between assets and liabilities in a foreign currency. We do not distinguish between monetary or non-monetary assets at this point: the ultimate translation effect on equity just has to conform to this difference. Whatever assets we have in pounds, less our liabilities in pounds, dictates the translation impact on equity from changes in GBP/USD. And this is exactly how it works out too. It is just that accounting rules make things more complicated by being very specific about which translation GLs are allowed to go into the net income statement and which are not. The CTGL is needed to bring about the necessary end result.

At this point we have established how to understand exposures at three different levels: commercial exposure, net income exposure, and balance sheet exposure. Management teams may differ in terms of how important they consider each of these exposures to be. We return in Chapter 9 to a discussion of how to prioritize among these different exposures and come up with a firm-wide policy for FXRM that is defensible from a shareholder value point of view. Our main message for now, regardless of which objective is ultimately viewed as more valid, is that any FXRM programme should rest on a solid understanding and quantification of exposures at all three levels. Only then can the appropriate trade-offs be made, and unintended consequences avoided.

Key Chapter Takeaways

➤ Translation gains and losses related to non-monetary assets and liabilities also have an impact on shareholders' equity.
➤ These impacts are not reported in net income, however, but rather in other comprehensive income. They accumulate in an equity account called the translation reserve.
➤ The translation gains and losses on non-monetary items are important to understand in order to avoid surprises and to be able to communicate balance sheet developments both internally and externally.
➤ The mechanism involving the other comprehensive income/translation reserve is also what reconciles the firm's financial statement when there are translation gains or losses on monetary assets and liabilities that are not reported in net income, which is the case when the transaction currency is the same as the functional currency.
➤ This mechanism is also what neutralizes the gains or losses on internal transactions, thus preventing them from having an impact on shareholders' equity.
➤ In the end, the overall sensitivity of shareholders' equity to translation effects is dictated by the firm's net asset–liability position, which is simply the difference between assets and liabilities denominated in a specific foreign currency, regardless of whether they are monetary or non-monetary.

Further Reading

Aabo, T., M. A. Hansen, and Y. G. Muradoglu. 2015. Foreign debt usage in non-financial firms: A horse race between operating and accounting exposure hedging. *European Financial Management* **21**, 590–611.

Eiteman, K. D., A. I. Stonehill, and M. H. Moffett. 2015. *Multinational Business Finance* (14th edn). Pearson Education: Harlow.

Chapter 5
FX Derivatives Explained

Derivatives are financial instruments whose value derives from an underlying reference variable or price. Today, thanks to financial engineering, the underlying can be almost anything: movie revenues, the weather, or freight rates are just some examples. The bulk of derivative contracts, though, are written on prices or rates observable in the financial markets, such as stock prices, interest rates, and – of course – foreign exchange rates. The price of an FX derivative therefore depends on the value of a specific exchange rate. As the value of the exchange rate fluctuates, the price of the derivative will change according to the specific pricing formula that links the two.

Surveys of corporations show that a significant majority of firms with exposure to exchange rates use FX derivatives. They are used either to manage risk, or to take speculative views on markets. Many strongly associate FXRM with derivatives, almost to the point where the two become synonymous. We disagree with this view. While derivatives are often an integral part of FXRM, they are only one way of managing FX risk. Equally important to consider are natural hedges[1] and the currency composition of corporate assets

---

[1] By creating natural hedges we mean changing the FX composition of commercial cash flows through changing processes related to sales and purchases.

and liabilities, not least debt. Furthermore, derivatives are usually limited in that they are only able to influence the risk profile in the short to medium term, whereas firms often have projects that span decades.

The main advantage of derivatives as a tool for FXRM lies in their flexibility and versatility in managing a risk–return profile. The way to think about them is as building blocks that can be assembled in different ways to create exactly the desired risk–return profile over a specific time horizon. While this sounds attractive, we also need to consider that derivatives come with significant administrative costs and other drawbacks. History has also taught us that derivatives, wrongly applied, do not control risks but actually magnify them – on a potentially company-wrecking scale. There is a long list of derivative scandals where enormous losses have been the consequence, sometimes to the point of crushing the company (think of Barings Bank in 1995 or Metallgesellschaft in 1993). It is for these reasons that Warren Buffet has described derivatives as 'financial weapons of mass destruction'. It should therefore be recognized that using derivatives requires a deep understanding of the company's risk profile and the potential effects it has on cash flow and net income across a wide range of scenarios.

We will divide FX derivatives into three categories: forward/futures, swaps, and options. The first two are examples of derivatives whose payoff is essentially a linear function of the underlying exchange rate, whereas options are derivatives where the payoff function is non-linear and depends on the exchange rates in more complicated ways. Options, in turn, can be divided into 'vanilla' and 'exotic', where the former refers to the simplest and most commonly used types of options, the bread-and-butter of the option market. The exotics are a large and disparate group of instruments whose payoff functions and pricing formulas are potentially very complex. They are not covered in this book. Our recommendation is to steer clear of the exotics unless a very convincing case can be made. As a general rule, firms do well to stick to transparent and simple derivatives for which liquid markets exist.

The Basics of Forward Contracts

An FX forward contract is one in which the participants agree on an exchange rate for a specific date in the future, say three, six, or nine months out. That is, it is about fixing *now* the exchange rate that will apply to a transaction at some point *in the future*.

The classical example is a producer who sells his or her goods on export and thereby creates a receivable in foreign currency. The receivable is due at a certain date ($t = n$), and the producer wants to eliminate the uncertainty about the exchange rate on that date. The producer therefore enters a forward contract that effectively allows a locking in of the current forward rate. So, instead of getting the uncertain spot rate at $t = n$ the producer ensures that they can convert the receivable with the forward rate available today ($t = 0$). We will denote the spot rate as S, and the forward rate as F. We will indicate both the start date and maturity of the forward contract. For example, $F_{(0, 1)}$ indicates a one-year forward contract where the rate is locked in today ($t = 0$). So, using notation and assuming that the receivable is due in six months, the exporter replaces the unknown future spot rate six months hence ($S_{0.5}$) with the known six-month forward rate available today ($F_{(0, 0.5)}$), thereby eliminating uncertainty about the value of the receivable in home currency terms.

The producer who locks in a forward rate is said to be *selling forward*. More specifically, if the producer is a German firm exporting to the USA, the firm is selling US dollars forward. This terminology comes from the fact that the company will normally, once the receivable is settled, be selling the dollars it receives in the market to convert them into euros. We can also turn the example around and analyse it from the perspective of an importing firm, who in this case is sourcing goods priced in US dollars. Such an organization may want to ensure that it locks in the price at which it can buy US dollars on the day the payable is due for payment, because it will need dollars on that day to pay the supplier. This is referred to as *buying forward*.

So, in each FX forward transaction one party is always selling a currency forward, and the other buying the same currency forward. This is by necessity a zero-sum game (i.e. what one gains is a loss to the other). Because of our convention of quoting exchange rates as the number of home currency units for one unit of foreign currency, the payoff can be written $(F - S)$ for the party selling forward. It gains if the spot rate at maturity turns out to be lower than the forward price it has locked in. The payoff is exactly the opposite for the party buying forward: $(S - F)$.

To exemplify forward payoffs, let us say that the German exporter is able to lock in a forward rate of 0.9 through a contract that matures in six months and has a nominal amount of US$1 mn. When the contract is settled, the actual USD/EURO rate turns out to be 0.8. This represents a weaker dollar and a loss on the receivable. The producer, however, has protected him or herself against this outcome because the payoff from the forward contract will be $(0.9 - 0.8) * 1,000,000 = €100,000$. The total cash flow is $0.8 * 1,000,000 + 100,000 = €900,000$ (the cash flow from the receivable plus the payoff on the forward contract). In fact, the outcome of €900,000 is guaranteed. If the spot rate ends up being 0.95 instead, the exporter makes a loss on the contract. The loss can be calculated as $(0.9 - 0.95) * 1,000,000 = -€50,000$, which, put together with the cash flow from the receivable $(0.95 * 1,000,000)$, adds up to €900,000.

The linear payoff structure of a forward contract is shown in Figure 5.1 (exporter perspective, i.e. selling forward strategy). Panel A illustrates the payoff of the contract itself, whereas Panel B shows the payoff in terms of the firm's hedged revenue (revenue + payoff from derivative), assuming that 100% of the receivable is covered.[2]

---

[2] Normally the payoff from FX derivatives would be reported in financial expenses and not be included in revenue. We use the term 'hedged revenue' only to illustrate the combined effect.

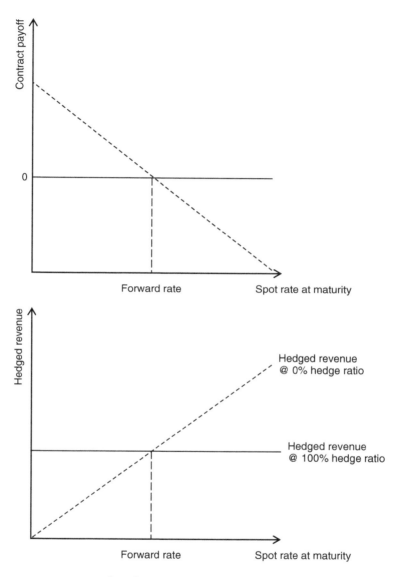

Figure 5.1   Payoff FX forward (sold forward)

Determining Forward Rates

How are forward rates determined? Forward rates are essentially determined by money-market rates. There are three elements involved: the spot exchange rate between currencies A and B, the interest rate in currency A, and the interest rate in currency B. In fact, once we know the spot rate it is only a matter of applying the difference between the two interest rates to derive the forward price.

The key to getting forward pricing right is the insight that any currency that offers a higher interest rate must be expected to weaken relative to the spot rate. Consider the case where the USD/SEK is currently 9.0 and the US short-term interest rate is 3% while the Swedish rate is only 2% (annualized rates). This 1% differential makes it more attractive to keep money invested in US dollars. The forward price is set so as to compensate anyone who invests in Swedish interest-bearing instruments for the lower interest rate. In this case, the forward price of US dollars in Swedish krona terms must be lower than the spot price in order to preserve neutrality between the strategies of investing in US dollars and Swedish krona. That is, the forward rate must indicate a weaker dollar than the spot rate. If the US interest rate is higher *and* the forward rate indicates a strengthening US dollar, it would be too easy to make a fortune by investing in US interest-bearing instruments while simultaneously locking in the forward rate. In fact, nobody would invest in Swedish krona.

Let us introduce some more notation to formalize these ideas. Denote the annualized interest rates as r_H and r_F, where H stands for the home country interest rate and F stands for the foreign currency. The Swedish krona is considered the home currency, since the exchange rate in our example is expressed as USD/SEK. The difference, denoted r^*, is calculated as $(r_H - r_F)$. Then we use the difference to derive the forward rate as $F_{(0, n)} = S_0 * (1 + r^H)/(1 + r^F)$. Continuing the example, if the contract has a maturity of one year the forward rate would be calculated as $9 * (1.02)/(1.03) = 8.9126$. This forward rate agrees with our intuition: to compensate for the higher US interest rate, the forward rate must be lower than the spot rate, consistent with a weaker US dollar (fewer krona needed to buy one dollar = weaker dollar).

The rates used in forward contracts are, like all derivatives, set to prevent arbitrage, which is to say risk-free gains. To see how arbitrage works, recall that the 1% differential in the example above makes it more attractive to keep money invested in US dollars. If we are able to write FX forward contracts using, say, 9.0 as forward rate instead, it is easy to make a risk-free gain. Just borrow money in Swedish krona at 2%, convert that into dollars at 9.0, invest the money at 3%, and simultaneously enter a forward contract to convert it back to krona after six months at 9.0. If we borrow 9 mn krona, getting US$1 mn to invest, this generates $1,000,000 * 1.03 = 1,030,000$ if invested at 3% for one year. When we convert this back to krona at the forward rate of 9.0, we get 9,270,000 krona. At the same time, we owe the bank $9,000,000 * 1.02 = 9,180,000$ krona for having borrowed money during these 12 months. We repay the bank this amount, pocketing a gain of 90,000 krona at zero risk. In efficient financial markets, this kind of arbitrage is not supposed to happen: money is not left on the table by rational investors.

While understanding how forward rates are set is important, we should not lose sight of the fact that entering an FX contract means creating a receivable in one currency and a payable in another. This is a major takeaway from an FXRM perspective. Nothing prevents a Swedish firm, for example, from being party to an FX forward in which US dollars are sold forward against the euro, or any other foreign currency for which a market exists. Let us say it does so at a USD/EUR rate of 0.869 for US$1 mn. This means that, effectively, the firm will pay US$1 mn and receive €0.869 mn when that contract matures. What has been fixed is just the USD/EUR exchange rate. From a krona perspective, in which corporate performance is measured, the company now has two transactions (one receivable and one payable) affecting their net transaction exposure to the US dollar and the euro, respectively.

FX Futures Contracts

FX futures are very similar to FX forward contracts. An exchange rate is fixed at a future date for a specific amount of currency. There are some important differences, however, that we will explore in this section.

One major difference is that futures are standardized contracts trading on an exchange, whereas forwards are negotiated 'over the counter' (OTC). This means that the contract details are negotiated bilaterally between two parties, say a bank and a manufacturing company. Any aspect of the deal is up for negotiation, and can therefore be tailored to suit the needs of the players involved. Because it is a bilateral agreement, credit risk is a real concern in a forward contract. In a futures contract, however, the exchange acts as counterparty to both sides of the trade, taking counterparty risk out of the equation for investors. The exchange also provides clearing and settlement of the outstanding amounts when the contract is due for payment. In return for lower counterparty risk, the participants in the trade give up flexibility. A futures contract leaves no scope for customization of the contract. Rather, the terms in a futures contract, such as rate, nominal amount, and maturity, are fixed.

To participate in a trade on a futures exchange it is necessary to post collateral in the form of cash or a credit line guaranteed by a bank. This is the other main difference between a future and a forward contract. The purpose of the collateral, referred to as maintenance margin, is to reduce counterparty credit risk from the perspective of the exchange. In the early days of trading, the individual on the losing end of a contract might simply walk away from it. The margin requirement was introduced by the exchanges as a way to deal with this problem: anyone walking out on the deal loses his or her collateral.

These aspects make futures popular with investors seeking to make leveraged bets on exchange rates. From a pure trading perspective, futures look very different. Unlike forwards, a future does not involve physical settlement, which is to say actually exchanging the nominal currency amounts when the contract matures. It is a derivative whose value is marked-to-market on a daily basis and then settled on a net basis at maturity. Because of this feature, it is in fact a leveraged position in a currency, which is what attracts certain investors. The upfront investment is just the margin, which is a small fraction of the nominal amounts that would be exchanged in a forward contract. If the margin requirement is 10%, an investor would only have to fund an initial investment of US$10 mn on a contract involving a nominal amount of US$100 mn. After that initial investment is made, the investor gains or loses according to the daily revaluations of the position, which reflect the full nominal amount of US$100 mn. It is because of this feature that a futures contract is viewed as a leveraged position in the underlying. The leverage of course makes the position riskier.

The margin requirement has some important implications for FXRM. It turns out that the initial margin deposited is not the whole story. In fact, the size of the collateral that is required changes dynamically with the size of the unrealized gain or loss. Every day the position is valued anew, or, in the jargon, 'marked-to-market'. If the loss exceeds a pre-agreed threshold, the firm is called on to post additional collateral to keep the counterparty risk acceptable to the exchange. This is referred to as a *margin call*, and basically means that the firm needs to inject extra liquidity into their trading account to compensate for the added credit risk that builds up as unrealized losses accumulate.

In our experience, margin calls definitely complicate liquidity management and add to the administrative burden of a company. The derivative is normally entered into with the purpose of hedging a specific transaction at some future point in time. The margin calls create interim cash effects that are hard to predict, and for which, importantly, there is no offsetting effect from the underlying exposure being hedged. The firm simply must have the money around just in case a margin call occurs.[3] And the amounts involved can be staggering, especially for contracts with longer maturities.

---

[3] It should be noted that margin calls are two-way: the company stands to receive cash injections if the exchange rate moves in the other direction.

The need to manage margin calls means that firms should approach futures contracts with caution. The havoc that they can wreak on a firm's liquidity planning means they are best avoided unless the firm has substantial cash resources at hand. Another circumstance to keep in mind is that futures contracts are large: the nominal amounts on offer are typically out of range for a sizeable fraction of operating firms. The lack of flexibility in setting the contract terms is also a reason why many firms prefer to use forward contracts where the terms can be negotiated.

Currency Swaps

Currency swaps are an important part of the FXRM toolbox. They allow firms to swap cash flows in one currency into another currency over longer time horizons than what is normally available for FX forwards or futures. The cash flows in a swap normally, but not always, correspond to the interest payments and principal in an existing loan. We refer to it as an interest rate swap when both legs in the swap are in the same currency, and a currency swap when at least one of them is in a foreign currency. Currency swaps got started in the 1970s because firms wanted to bypass the regulations on cross-border transactions that existed at the time in western economies.

Swaps are OTC deals and can therefore be customized. Nothing prevents two firms from entering a swap directly with each other, but these days swap dealers (normally a large global bank) are usually engaged as a counterparty to the swap transaction. The basic structure of an interest rate swap is fixed-to-floating or floating-to-fixed, where the floating rate leg is based on the relevant 3-month reference rate (normally LIBOR-London Interbank Offered Rate). With a currency swap the possibilities multiply, because the choice of currency is added to both legs of the swap. But a swap can be varied in more ways. For example, the participants may agree to exclude the notional amount and only swap the interest payments.

Swaps are used extensively by firms, both as a way to minimize their financing costs and to manage their risk exposures. For example, a company currently paying a fixed rate on its loan may believe that interest rates are going down. Therefore, they wish to enter into a swap that lets them receive fixed-rate payments and pay the floating rate. The fixed-rate payments received under the swap agreement cancel out the fixed-rate payments paid on the loan. By using a swap, the company effectively ends up exposed to the short-term interest rate despite having initially borrowed at a fixed rate. Having a policy that targets a specific fixed/floating rate mix for the loan portfolio, or taking a view on interest rate developments, are common motivations behind swaps.

Swaps, like any derivative, are versatile tools for expressing views on markets. They also have an economic rationale, however: a currency swap gives firms a chance to borrow in the home market yet still achieve their desired FX exposure. Firms usually have a comparative advantage in borrowing in their home market because they have a relationship with one or more of the local banks, which reduces information asymmetries and transaction costs. For this reason, the interest rate they can obtain is lower than what they would have got if they had borrowed abroad where they are less known to the investor community. But perhaps the firm would prefer to have the loan in foreign currency in order to match expenses with sales it generates in that currency. This is where currency swaps come into the picture.

To exemplify a currency swap, let us say a UK firm borrows £100 mn in a five-year loan from its house bank, paying a fixed interest rate of 6%. However, it has an exposure to the US dollar from regularly converting the dividends it receives from a US-based subsidiary. To offset this exposure, it wishes to swap its debt payment into dollars and therefore contacts a swap dealer. The parties agree to a fixed–fixed swap contract with a notional amount of £100 mn. The notional amount in US dollar terms is US$130 mn, reflecting an implicit GBP/USD spot rate of 1.3. Under the contract terms, the UK firm, at inception, receives US$130 mn from the swap dealer immediately, whereas the swap dealer is paid £100 mn (an exchange of the nominal amount). The UK firm then pays US$6.5 mn annually, corresponding to a fixed rate of 5% in dollar terms, but at the same time receives £100 mn * 6% = £6 mn every year for five years. At the end of the five-year contract, the nominal amounts are exchanged back. Note that, from the UK firm's perspective, the cash flow stream it receives exactly cancels out the payments it needs to make to its bank under the original loan agreement. In contrast, the cash flow stream it pays mimics taking up and eventually repaying a fixed interest rate loan in US dollars, serviced by its dollar dividend stream.

A couple of things are worth noting about currency swaps. One is that while the cash flows from the swap mirror actual loans in the foreign currency, the firm keeps the original loan and is responsible for making both interest payments and instalments on it. Swaps do not add funding to the firm. They are a way to reconfigure the firm's mix of interest rate and currency exposure on its liabilities without having to incur new ones. This is one of the things about swaps that are appealing to firms, since the alternative would have been to actually take up a new loan in a foreign currency, which would provide more funding, which the firm may not be in need of.

Just like FX futures, swaps may complicate liquidity management to the extent that collateral is needed to cover unrealized losses. While weaker firms (with ratings below investment grade) are normally excluded from the swap market altogether, it has become more common to write margin requirements into swaps even for relatively creditworthy firms. The upshot is that a firm may find itself having to inject additional liquidity, over and above the scheduled payments in the swap, as a result of unrealized losses (when the market value of the swap is negative).[4]

From an FXRM viewpoint, we can think of currency swaps as a series of FX forwards. As such, swaps are a string of receivables

---

[4] As with futures contracts, the margin calls are two-way and the firm stands to receive cash injections if the market value is positive.

in one currency and a string of payables in another. In fact, any linear derivative that refers to an exchange rate can (and should) be expressed as a portfolio of receivables/payables in order to be able to facilitate the calculation of the firm's overall exposure to that currency. This conclusion is not affected by the common practice of netting the cash flows of the two legs in the swap. That is, to limit counterparty risk, the gross cash payments indicated by the swap do not change hands. Instead, the net value of the two legs in the swap is calculated and only this amount is transferred. At the end of the day, though, what matters to get exposures right are the underlying receivables and payables.

From an exposure point of view, it should also be remembered that most currency swaps are composites of interest rate and currency risk. Unlike an FX forward, where only unrealized gains and losses are affected by changes in interest rates (due to the valuation required by fair value accounting, see Chapter 6), the actual cash flows of a currency swap will depend on the short-term interest rate (if at least one leg is floating rate). This calls for a more dynamic and integrated approach to exposure management, which is the topic of Chapter 8.

The Basics of FX Options

An FX option is a derivative that gives the holder the right, but not the obligation, to buy (or sell) a currency at a predetermined exchange rate. The exchange rate is the so-called 'underlying'; the price or rate to which the option refers and from which it derives its value.

There is a favourable asymmetry to options: the holder of the option will exercise her right to buy (or sell) only if it is profitable to do so. If not, she simply walks away from the contract without any payments having to be cash-settled. Thanks to the option feature, the payoff function of an option needs to be described by a maximum function. Below, K is the so-called strike price; the fixed exchange rate at which the holder can, but does not have to, exercise her option. S denotes the spot rate at maturity. The exact shape of the payoff function depends on whether it is a put or a call option.

- **Call option.** Gives the holder the right to buy a currency at the pre-agreed strike price. Payoff function: $\max(S - K; 0)$.
- **Put option.** Gives the holder the right to sell a currency at the pre-agreed strike price. Payoff function: $\max(K - S; 0)$.

To understand the payoff functions, it is helpful to begin by establishing the perspective of the hedging firm. At this point, recall that we express exchange rates in terms of units of home currency per one unit of foreign currency. When we say 'sell a currency' or 'buy a currency', we refer to the foreign currency. The home currency is always assumed to be the currency in which the hedging firm measures its performance.

Take, for example, the perspective of an exporter (a producing firm) based in Germany that sells goods and services on export to the US market. A put option in this case would be the right to sell US dollars at a certain strike price. From a commercial point of view, the euro-based exporter loses from a weaker dollar. This tells us that, to offset the commercial risk, the option must benefit from a weaker dollar. A weaker US dollar implies a *lower* USD/EUR exchange rate (it takes fewer units of euros to buy one dollar). Hence the payoff function of the put option: $\max(K - S; 0)$. The lower the USD/EUR spot rate, the weaker the dollar, and the larger the payoff on the option.

The basic payoff structure of a bought put option is shown in Figure 5.2 (exporter perspective). Panel A illustrates the payoff of the contract itself, whereas Panel B shows the payoff in terms of the firm's hedged revenue (revenue + payoff from derivative), assuming that 100% of the receivable is covered.[5]

Buying a put option in dollars (the right to sell) is an alternative to the strategy of selling dollars forward. Compare the payoff function of the put option with the forward contract: $\max(K - S; 0)$

---

[5] In actual practice, the payoff from any FX derivative would be booked in financial expenses and not revenue. The net effect would be the same as in the graph, however.

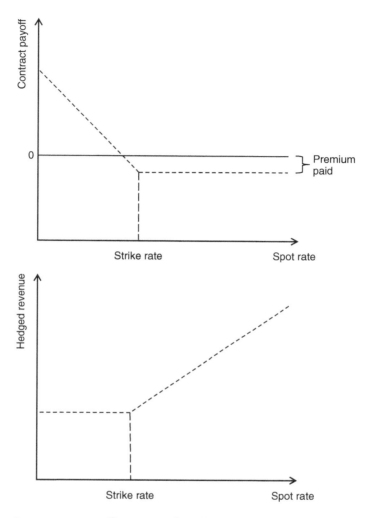

Figure 5.2 Payoff FX option (bought put)

vs $(F - S)$, respectively. The hedging firm benefits from a weaker dollar also in the case of a forward sale. But there is no favourable asymmetry here. Both parties to the forward contract must accept the possibility that they will have to pay the counterparty if the spot rate moves against them.

The right to walk away from unfavourable outcomes is obviously a privilege, for which the option holder needs to pay an upfront payment. This payment is referred to as the option premium. The premium must thus be large enough to induce the counterparty to accept the unfavourable asymmetry. How large the option premium should be is determined through an option valuation formula. While an option's value is sensitive to more factors, three model parameters stand out: the strike price, the volatility of the exchange rate, and the maturity of the contract.

- **Strike price closer to prevailing forward rate ⇒ higher option value.** An option for which it takes less movement in the exchange rate to reach the strike price offers more risk reduction.
- **More volatile exchange rate ⇒ higher option value.** More variability in the exchange rate means that there is a larger probability of reaching the strike price.
- **Longer contract maturity ⇒ higher option value.** A longer maturity gives the exchange rate a longer time over which to reach the strike price.

When the spot rate reaches the strike price, the option is said to be 'in-the-money' (i.e. it would be profitable for the holder of the option to exercise the option already today). For example, an option to sell US dollars at a strike price of USD/EUR 0.8 is in-the-money if the spot rate is 0.75 (the US dollar has weakened). If the spot rate is 0.85 instead, the option is 'out-of-the-money' and would render zero if exercised. But the key to understanding options is that they are not worthless just because they are out-of-the-money. As long as some time remains on the contract, there is a chance that the exchange rate will move so that the strike price is reached before expiry. This is called the 'time value' of options.[6] Especially the combination of a long maturity and high volatility in the exchange rate is powerful. Such options can fetch a high price even

---

[6] An option's value can be divided into two parts: option value = time value + intrinsic value. Intrinsic value refers to the payoff it would render if exercised immediately.

when they are out-of-the-money, because the long maturity–high volatility combination leads to a wide range of potential outcomes, and therefore a higher probability that the option will end up in-the-money before it expires.

It is also useful to be able to distinguish between the following three types of options:

- **European options.** Can only be exercised when the option matures.
- **American options.** Give the holder the right to exercise the option at any time before the expiry date.
- **Asian options.** The strike price is based on the average price in a given period, as opposed to the end-of-period spot rate.

From a corporate perspective, an American option has the advantage of being easy to convert into ready cash should the need arise (ahead of contract maturity). Corporates also sometimes show a preference for Asian-type put options, because they think the averaging corresponds better to the realization of commercial cash flows in the period. The cash flow realized from commercial transactions in foreign currency, for example, is not converted as a lump sum at quarter end but on an ongoing basis.

Options from an FXRM Point of View

Options offer managers another way to deal with FX risk compared to forwards/futures. Instead of locking in a future exchange rate, we establish a floor below which it cannot go (or a cap it cannot exceed, depending on whether we are an exporter or an importer). In option contracts we pay for the risk reduction by handing over a cash premium to the seller of the option. With a forward or futures contract, we instead pay by surrendering upside potential to the counterparty. While we have reduced our downside risk by entering the contract, we have also given up any upside potential that we would have had without it. Therefore, it is an illusion to think forward contracts are 'free' just because they involve no cash premium. Cashless? Yes. Free? No. Sacrificing upside potential is just a different way of paying for the privilege of risk reduction.

It is also important to see that the option premium paid is not a cost in the true sense of the word. The net present value of a fairly priced option should in fact be close to zero. It is more correct to view the option premium as an investment in a derivative asset. This is precisely what happens when the option is bought. Assume that a firm spends US$4 mn on a put option. The premium reduces the firm's cash balance by precisely that amount. But the firm simultaneously recognizes a derivative asset in its balance sheet amounting to US$4 mn. Total assets are therefore unchanged and there is no impact on book equity. Hence, the option is not a real cost. As with many other investments, the derivative asset depreciates over time as less and less time remains on the contract, thereby lowering its value.[7] If the exchange rate remains stable, the option gradually decreases in value by each period simply because it loses value from the passage of time.

When should firms prefer FX options over FX forwards? The academic literature does not provide very clear guidance on this issue, but some ideas have been suggested. One is that options allow firms to deal effectively with the problem of over-hedging. This problem occurs when the firm thinks it will receive a certain amount of foreign currency, and hedges the entire amount, only to find that the actual volume of business turned out to be less because business conditions changed. Because of their flexibility, options are an advantage in this situation. A type of situation in which a forward might be preferred is when the firm is financially constrained and finds it difficult to generate money for the cash premium. An option premium that reduces the amount the firm can spend on investment in real assets (its core business) is probably not an attractive proposition.

---

[7] This is not to say that the option cannot increase in value. If the exchange rate moves favourably from the viewpoint of the option, the derivative asset can of course go above US$4 mn, leading to unrealized and ultimately realized gains being recognized in net income. But it remains true that as less and less time remains on the contract, an out-of-the-money option will gradually lose value and become zero at maturity.

The so-called 'collar' is a common option strategy that allows a firm to compromise between the two extremes of sacrificing all upside (a forward/future) and paying a heavy option premium. For an exporting firm, a collar involves two positions. A bought put option, which serves the purpose of hedging the commercial risk exposure. To finance this put option the firm writes a sell option rather than paying with cash. When the firm writes the call option it receives a premium, which offsets the premium paid on the put. The 'cashless collar' is a special case where the strike prices are set so that the premiums on the two options exactly offset each other.

The basic payoff structure of a collar is shown in Figure 5.3 (exporter perspective). Panel A illustrates the payoff of the contract itself, whereas Panel B shows the payoff in terms of the firm's hedged revenue (revenue + payoff from derivative), assuming that 100% of the receivable is covered.

The popularity of the FX collar strategy can probably be put down to managers being averse to paying the put premium. The written call means that the firm misses out on some of the upside potential, but this is seen as a lesser evil, especially if the firm is cash-constrained. There is a case for such a view. Whereas the investors of an oil company, say, may be disappointed to learn that the firm has hedged away its upside potential to the oil price, investors rarely pick a stock just to get more exposure to a certain exchange rate. From this point of view, giving away some upside potential in the currency may be a more convenient and 'cheaper' way of financing the put option than using cash in hand.

In this section, we have reviewed basic, or 'vanilla', option strategies. Options come in an amazing variety, however, courtesy of financial engineering. We argue that such 'exotic' options do not have a role to play in an FXRM programme. The reasons are simple. The pricing of such options is not transparent because of the complexity, offering the provider rich opportunities to price in an attractive margin. Financial derivatives are not necessarily value-neutral at inception, contrary to what is sometimes heard, especially for complex and 'engineered' products that are traded OTC and where the institution promoting the product has an

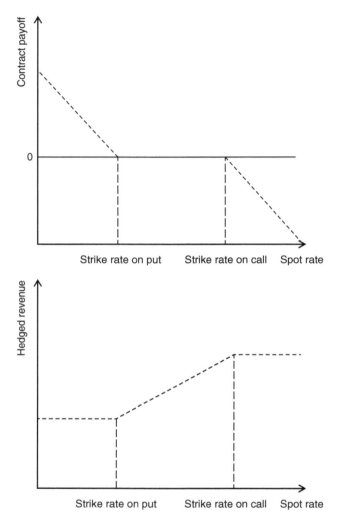

Figure 5.3 Payoff collar strategy

information advantage. The other reason to avoid exotics is that they make FXRM more complicated. Complexity is a liability in risk management. It increases the likelihood of surprises, or even disasters, simply from a lack of understanding. The more complex the product, the more difficult it will be to aggregate positions up to a meaningful and simple net number that informs management about the risk–return profile of the firm.

Key Chapter Takeaways

➤ Derivatives are a popular way of managing exposure to FX risk because they allow firms a great deal of flexibility in terms of adjusting the near-term risk profile.

➤ A major distinction is between derivatives where the payoff is a linear payoff of the underlying FX rate (such as forwards and swaps) and where the payoff is non-linear (options).

➤ An important consideration is whether the derivative position is subject to collateral requirements. Margin calls, which are when the counterparty requires additional collateral, can create surprises and greatly complicate liquidity management.

➤ Generally, a firm needs to pay for the protection against downside risk afforded by a derivative by paying an upfront cash premium (buying put options) or by sacrificing upside potential (e.g. in a forward or collar strategy).

➤ Firms are recommended to stay away from 'exotic' derivatives with complicated payoff functions. The complexity makes understanding net exposures more difficult, and the provider is likely to price in a larger margin than with liquid and transparent instruments.

➤ Derivatives come with several drawbacks, such as transaction costs, increased administration, and a potential for unintended effects because of being poorly understood.

Further Reading

Adam, T. R. 2002. Risk management and the credit risk premium. *Journal of Banking and Finance* **26**, 243–269.

Smith, S. W. 1996. Corporate risk management: Theory and practice. *Journal of Derivatives* **2**, 21–30.

Chapter 6
Hedge Accounting Explained

Most people like the idea behind derivatives, recognizing that they hold the potential to let firms flexibly fine-tune their risk–return profile. Derivative usage in practice, however, is beset by various complicating factors. One of these has to do with the way they are accounted for. Derivatives are fair value accounted, meaning, among other things, that firms need to recognize changes in the fair value of derivatives in net income. This is generally viewed as problematic. Managers worry that analysts do not like the excess volatility in profits caused by these fair value changes. The fluctuations in the value of derivative contracts can indeed be large, and the firm is not allowed to apply the same fair value accounting to the business transaction that they have hedged.

The conundrum is therefore that while the exposure may be perfectly hedged in the sense of protecting the cash flow in a commercial transaction, net income may in fact become more, not less, volatile because of these accounting conventions.

The solution on offer is called hedge accounting, which is regulated by the standards IFRS 9 and ASC 815 in US Generally

US GAAP. Hedge accounting is a technique for keeping the unrealized GLs out of net income until the hedge contract is realized (i.e. cash-settled at maturity). It lets firms achieve the desired outcome of stabilizing cash flow by hedging without having to worry about any unpredictable swings in net income as a side-effect.

If this sounds too good to be true, it often is. Hedge accounting is a costly and cumbersome process. It will call on highly skilled (and highly paid) individuals to devote significant time to documenting that the firm is in compliance with the requirements. It will create financial reports that are cluttered and nearly incomprehensible, as the jargon surrounding it is heavy and arcane.

Is hedge accounting worth the cost and effort? Answering this question comes down to whether one thinks the stock market, or other stakeholders, really punishes the firm for reporting potentially large unrealized GLs that make net income seem less stable. As previously discussed, net income is closely watched and often used as shorthand for corporate performance in the business community. If so, there might be a premium for keeping these GLs out of net income. This argument requires some rather strenuous assumptions, however, and can only be true if investors and analysts are unable to implement simple analytical adjustments. We argue that, by and large, this is not the case, and that the goal of avoiding any negative consequences of 'paper volatility' can often be obtained through improved communication.

Background

Derivatives are off-balance-sheet assets and liabilities. The meaning of 'off balance sheet' is that the firm is not required to show the nominal contract value in its balance sheet (as one would do with debt, for example). However, derivatives do find their way onto corporate balance sheets. This is because the bodies governing the main accounting standards (US GAAP and International Financial Reporting Standards, IFRS) have decided that derivatives are to be fair value accounted. Fair value accounting (FVA) means that assets and liabilities are carried in the balance sheet at their fair value. FVA is often contrasted with historical cost accounting, according to which ALs are carried at the original investment less accumulated depreciation/amortization. The latter method is completely detached from any actual price the asset would fetch in a market transaction. The philosophy behind the drive towards FVA is that fair values are more informative for investors and other stakeholders than historical cost estimates.

In the accounting standards, fair value is taken to mean the price that a rational and well-informed buyer and seller would agree on in an arm's-length transaction. It is often approximated with market values whenever those are available. In the case of derivatives, fair value is normally calculated using a specific valuation formula. At each balance sheet date, the firm has to 'mark-to-market' (i.e. value) its positions and report the net value as either an asset or a liability (depending on whether the net is positive or negative). It is therefore the value of the derivative contract, not its notional amount, that appears in the balance sheet.

The reason why derivatives are now accounted for on a fair value basis is that the rule-makers were concerned there was too little transparency about how these derivatives impacted firms' financial standing. In the past, firms were taking certain liberties in using derivatives to smooth net income over time. They might report a gain when it was to their advantage to do so, but choose not to report it when there was an unrealized loss. That is, negative outcomes on derivatives were opportunistically hidden from view.

We can compare the fair value accounting of derivatives with how a business transaction is accounted for. Accounting rules do not generally allow firms to capitalize an expected cash flow and put it on the balance sheet. It is only when the sale is invoiced that the deal is finally recognized by the accountants as a receivable or payable. The derivative is a recognizable event from day one, however, and therefore becomes subject to the accounting standards immediately.

There is thus a mismatch between the accounting treatment of derivatives and the business transactions they are supposed to hedge. Because of this fact, the fair value changes of the derivative will affect net income all the way from inception until the contract matures without a corresponding entry related to the anticipated cash flow being hedged. Especially early on in the derivative's life the fluctuations in value can be substantial, because a lot of time remains on the contract which makes it sensitive to assumptions about the future. The upshot is that one trades a decrease in cash flow risk for more net income volatility. Hedge accounting is meant to solve this problem.

Cash Flow vs Fair Value Hedging

In hedge accounting, there are two basic types of strategies: cash flow hedging and fair value hedging. They differ mainly in terms of what the objective of the hedge is.

- **Cash flow hedging.** The goal is to protect the cash flow related to a specific business transaction from the adverse impact of market risk.
- **Fair value hedging.** The goal is to protect the value of a specific asset or liability from the adverse impact of market risk.

Note that the terms cash flow hedging and fair value hedging refer to the economic rationale of the hedging strategy itself; that is, the question of why we want, from an economic point of view, to hedge in the first place. The ultimate purpose of hedge accounting, in contrast, depends on whether we are talking about cash flow or fair value hedging.

- The purpose of hedge accounting, as it relates to cash flow hedging, is to protect the firm's **net income** from the effect of unrealized GLs created by the derivative.

- The purpose of hedge accounting, as it relates to fair value hedging, is to protect the firm's **equity** from the effect of unrealized GLs created by the derivative.[1]

These are the benefits of hedge accounting from the firm's perspective: two of the key bottom lines (net income or equity) can be protected from the impact of unrealized GLs related to fair value accounting of derivatives.

A special case is **net investment hedging**. This refers to a situation where a firm borrows in a specific currency to neutralize the translation risk arising from a foreign subsidiary.[2] This can be said to protect the equity of the subsidiary (or the firm's 'net investment' in it – hence the terminology). A net investment hedge allows the firm to avoid reporting the gains or losses from the loan in net income, which it is normally required to do under accounting rules.

Corporate managers are for the most part interested in cash flow hedging. They are dealing with a continuous stream of cash flows and try to manage the potential impact of market risk on those. But fair value and net investment hedging are not uncommon in practice, so all three cases will be reviewed in this chapter.

Cash Flow Hedging: Basic Principles

A cash flow hedge serves the purpose of helping firms avoid the net income volatility that results from unrealized GLs on derivatives that are used to hedge commercial transactions. As discussed, firms may have legitimate reasons to hedge away FX risk on anticipated cash flows but be disinclined to report the unrealized GLs from the derivative in net income. It can be said that hedge accounting restores the matching principle since, if applied, the only impact from the hedge on net income will occur at maturity when the commercial transaction is also realized.

---

[1] Although, as we shall see, a fair value hedge will also reduce net income volatility. In some firms, this objective is as important, or even more so, than the objective of protecting equity. Banks that are managing their assets and liabilities so as to stay within minimum solvency targets may be chiefly concerned with the impact on equity from hedging strategies, whereas non-financial firms may more often cite protecting net income as being the main purpose.

[2] A derivative may also be used for this purpose.

For this to work, the unrealized GL will have to be reported differently compared to how accounting standards would normally have it. It remains the case that a derivative is always fair value accounted (i.e. it will be subjected to a valuation and the calculated value put on the balance sheet). When the value of a derivative asset increases (decreases), by definition a gain (loss) has to be recorded somewhere. Changes in assets and liabilities *must* be reflected in equity, since it is the net of the two. Net income normally is the channel through which this takes place: the GL is reported as income, which in turn increases or decreases the equity account 'retained earnings' accordingly.

Under hedge accounting, however, the unrealized GLs are instead placed in a different income statement, which we met in Chapter 4: other comprehensive income (OCI). OCI offers a different route for GLs to affect equity, thus bypassing net income. Whereas net income relates to the equity account retained earnings, OCI is instead linked to one called the 'hedging reserve', which is part of other reserves in equity.[3]

The mechanism of sending unrealized GLs on derivatives through the OCI/hedging reserve, rather than net income/retained earnings, is sometimes referred to as 'storing' GLs in reserves until contract settlement, at which time they are 'released' into net income.[4]

Hedge Accounting: An Example

To explain how hedge accounting works, we will use some examples. To understand the tables below, a bit of terminology is needed. Table 6.1 lists the accounts that are used in the examples

---

[3] From Chapter 4 we know that the account translation reserve is part of other reserves. Now we add the hedging reserve. That is, other reserves = translation reserve + hedging reserve. Other reserves may consist of more accounts, such as a revaluation reserve, but these are not discussed in this book.

[4] We remind the reader that some accountants prefer to view the unrealized gains and losses as hitting equity (the hedging reserve) directly, to then just be compiled and shown in other comprehensive income, as opposed to being actual income. This is of course semantics, and it does not matter to the outcome which perspective is preferred.

Table 6.1 Financial statement accounts

Asset	A:	Derivative assets
		Net assets in subsidiaries
		Cash
Liabilities	L:	Derivative liabilities
		Bond
Equity:	E:	Retained earnings
		Hedging reserve
		Translation reserve
Net income	NI:	Unrealized derivative GL
		Realized derivative GL
		Total derivative GL
Other comprehensive income	OCI:	Unrealized derivative GL
Cash flow statement	CFS:	Derivative cash flow

and their shorthand letters: A = assets; L = liabilities; E = equity; NI = net income; OCI = other comprehensive income; CFS = cash flow statement. The sign conventions are as follows. Positive numbers for assets, liabilities, and equity (though both cash and equity can assume negative values in case of losses). Positive sign for gains and negative for losses. The italics in the statement indicate that these items sum to the line that appears just below them. In all examples we ignore the effect of the business transaction being hedged, focusing instead on the mechanics of the derivative position. We also simplify away tax effects.

The goal is to understand the interplay between the two different ways of reconciling the asset and liability accounts with equity: OCI/hedging reserve (hedge accounting) and net income/retained earnings (no hedge accounting).

Table 6.2 refers to a German-based firm hedging a £90 mn anticipated sale that is expected 6 months from now (20X7.06.30). They lock in a GBP/EUR forward rate of 1.40. At inception the value of the hedge contract is zero and it therefore does not show up in the accounts. At 20X7.03.30 the pound has weakened to 1.35, such that the market value of the contract is €4.5 mn. At 20X7.06.30 the GBP/EUR has fallen even further to 1.33 such that the realized

Table 6.2 FX forward: hedge accounting *vs* no hedge accounting

		Panel 1: No hedge accounting of FX forward		Panel 2: Hedge accounting of FX forward	
		20X7.03.30	20X7.06.30	20X7.06.30	20X7.03.30
A:	Derivative assets	4.5	0	4.5	0
A:	Cash	0	6.3	0	6.3
L:	Derivative liabilities	0	0	0	0
E:	Retained earnings	4.5	6.3	0	6.3
E:	Hedging reserve	0	0	4.5	0
NI:	Unrealized derivative GL	4.5	−4.5	0	0
NI:	Realized derivative GL	0	6.3	0	6.3
NI:	Total derivative GL	4.5	1.8	0	6.3
CI:	Unrealized derivative GL	0	0	4.5	−4.5
CFS:	Derivative cash flow	0	6.3	0	6.3

payoff is €6.3 mn. The outcome is shown both with and without hedge accounting.[5]

A few things are worth noting. The scenario is one of a weaker pound (it takes fewer euros to buy one pound in the last period). A weaker pound is bad from the point of view of the commercial transaction, because the firm will receive fewer euros for its pound receivable. The hedge produces an offsetting effect, so it must be an unrealized gain at 20X7.03.30 and a realized gain at 20X7.06.30.

Regardless of accounting choice, the fair value of the derivative is €4.5 mn at 20X7.03.30, which will be reported as an asset. There is no cash flow yet as the contract has not been cash-settled. Therefore, the firm reports an unrealized gain of €4.5 mn. In the case of no hedge accounting, this fair value gain is shown as an unrealized derivative GL in net income, which is also the total derivative GL in that quarter. This gain leads to an increase in the firm's retained earnings, which closes the gap between assets and liabilities, on the one hand, and equity, on the other. In the case of hedge accounting, the €4.5 mn unrealized gain is instead shown as part of OCI. But this too serves to make the balance sheet balance, because it boosts another equity account, the hedging reserve.

On 20X7.06.30 the firm closes out its hedge at a gain of €6.3 mn. Since the derivative is settled in cash, the firm reports the same amount as a cash flow, which increases the firm's cash balance. The derivative asset ceases to exists at the maturity of the contract, at which point it is converted into a cash asset (whereas a liability would of course decrease cash instead).

The overall addition to the firm's assets is €6.3 mn, which must therefore also be the total gain related to the hedge as well. The firm recognizes a *realized* gain of €6.3 mn upon settlement. But €4.5 mn has already been recognized as an unrealized gain in the previous period, so this would overstate the total gain. Therefore, the previously reported unrealized gain is *reversed* when the

---

[5] We remind the reader that this kind of gross reporting of unrealized vs unrealized effects is not normally done in financial reports, but modelling it this way analytically helps us keep track of how the end result comes about.

contract is settled, which leads to a total derivative gain of €1.8 mn for the quarter. Because €4.5 mn has already been reported as an unrealized gain, thus adding that amount to equity, the total gain over the lifespan of the hedge is now 4.5 + 1.8 = €6.3mn, which corresponds to the increase in assets.

All in all, the effect on cash flow, assets, and equity is identical in the two cases. The difference lies solely in how the unrealized GLs are kept in the interim. The ultimate result is a €6.3 mn increase in assets and therefore also in equity. Under hedge accounting, however, the unrealized gain is 'stored' in the hedging reserve at 20X7.03.30 and not 'released' into net income until the contract reaches maturity (which should coincide with the commercial transaction, though this is not shown in the example).

Fair Value Hedge: An Example

The ultimate purpose of fair value hedge accounting is to protect and stabilize the firm's equity, while it simultaneously lowers the variability in net income. Consider a firm that has issued a fixed-rate bond in a foreign currency as part of its FXRM. At some point it wishes to pay the floating rate in that currency instead. It would then enter a swap agreement under which it receives the fixed rate and pays the floating rate. The fixed rate paid on the bond and the fixed rate received under the swap cancel each other out. Cash-flow-wise, the firm now has an exposure to the short-term interest rate. There is no economic exposure, however, in the sense that changes in the interest rate could cause a value effect on the firm's long-term fixed interest rate commitments. The value of the bond and the fixed-rate leg of the swap have the same sensitivity to interest rates and the firm is therefore neutral in that respect.

A swap is considered a derivative, however, and will therefore be fair value accounted, whereas the bond is not. This means that any fair value GLs on the swap will be shown in net income and therefore impact equity. This is the mismatch that hedge accounting addresses.

To exemplify, we will use a similar setup as in the preceding section. The only differences are that we add one line (the bond in the liability category) and the derivative lines now refer to a swap rather than an FX forward.

In Table 6.3 we depict a German-based firm that has issued a £25 mn fixed-rate bond in pounds sterling on 30 March. The GBP/EUR exchange rate at the time was 1.60, giving a nominal value in euro terms of €40 mn in the balance sheet. While the purpose of this bond issue is to finance an investment in real assets, we assume that the money is parked as cash (in euros) for the time being. The firm then immediately enters into a swap agreement under which it receives the fixed rate and pays the three-month UK Libor rate. It is thus value-neutral with respect to the long-term fixed-rate cash flows. At inception, the value of the swap is zero, so the lines for derivative assets and derivative liabilities are both zero.

By the time the firm closes its book for the second quarterly report, UK interest rates have come down. This is a bad scenario from the point of view of the firm, because the bond increases in value by €5 mn.[6] This loss is not reported in net income, however, since the bond is not fair value accounted. The swap gains in value correspondingly. Because it is fair value accounted, however, the €5 mn gain generated by the swap goes through net income. In Table 6.3, Panel 1 shows how this impacts the equity of the firm in the absence of hedge accounting. To balance the books in light of the €5 mn derivative asset, net income and retained earnings both increase by the same amount. The swap has therefore created volatility in both these accounts.

Panel 2 in Table 6.3 shows the outcome when hedge accounting is implemented. In this case, the firm is allowed to add the €5 mn value increase to the bond's carrying value, which is now €45 mn compared to €40 mn without hedge accounting. As a result, the change in value on the swap and the bond balance out and there is no net effect on equity (the higher bond value increases liabilities but the derivative asset increases assets by the same amount).

---

[6] Changes in interest rates are likely to also have an impact on the exchange rate. We leave exchange rate assumptions out of the example to simplify the exposition.

Table 6.3 FX swap: hedge accounting vs no hedge accounting

Panel 1: No hedge accounting of FX swap

		20X7.03.30	20X7.06.30
A:	Derivative assets	0	5
A:	Cash	40	40
L:	Bond	40	40
L:	Derivative liabilities	0	0
E:	Retained earnings	0	5
E:	Hedging reserve	0	0
NI:	Unrealized derivative GL	0	5
NI:	Realized derivative GL	0	0
NI:	Total derivative GL	0	5
CI:	Unrealized derivative GL	0	0
CFS:	Derivative cash flow	0	0

Panel 2: Hedge accounting of FX swap

		20X7.06.30	20X7.03.30
A:	Derivative assets	0	5
A:	Cash	40	40
L:	Bond	40	45
L:	Derivative liabilities	0	0
E:	Retained earnings	0	0
E:	Hedging reserve	0	0
NI:	Unrealized derivative GL	0	0
NI:	Realized derivative GL	0	0
NI:	Total derivative GL	0	0
CI:	Unrealized derivative GL	0	0
CFS:	Derivative cash flow	0	0

It is worth noting that while technically the firm applied hedge accounting on the derivative (the swap), it is the carrying value of the bond that adjusts. One may think of this as the fair value GL on the swap being simultaneously added to both the asset and the liability side of the balance sheet, leaving equity unaffected.

As a side note, one may reflect on the accuracy of referring to swaps and other derivatives as hedges. It is unclear to what extent derivatives really is applied as hedges in the proper sense of the word. Some companies are known to change the mix of currencies and floating vs fixed-rate liabilities purely in an attempt to improve corporate performance rather than as proper risk management tools as defined in this book. Regardless of the actual motivation behind using derivatives, an FX risk manager must be knowledgeable about how any such transactions affect the reported financials.

Net Investment Hedge: An Example

A net investment hedge refers to a situation where a firm has a foreign subsidiary and wishes to hedge the resulting translation risk by borrowing in the same currency. If the foreign currency depreciates, there will be a translation loss on the subsidiary's net assets, but the firm will register an offsetting translation gain on the loan (which is now worth less in home-currency terms).

How does hedge accounting come into the picture? Hedge accounting is always motivated by a mismatch in the accounting standards that apply for the hedged item and the hedging instrument. In this case, the mismatch arises because the investment in the subsidiary (the hedged item) is not a monetary asset, whereas the loan (the hedge) is a monetary liability. Recall from Chapter 3 that the translation GLs on monetary ALs are to be reported in net income. The result of borrowing in the same currency as the subsidiary, while it stabilizes equity due to lowering the net AL position, is therefore more volatility in net income. Many firms find this undesirable and opt for hedge accounting of the loan, which allows them to show the translation GLs in OCI instead.

Table 6.4 illustrates a net investment hedge. Because we are not actually speaking about derivatives here (the hedge is the loan in this case, and a loan is not considered a derivative), those lines are no longer needed. The situation refers to a firm with euros as its functional currency that has issued a US$20 mn bond to acquire a subsidiary with US dollars as the functional currency. At the time (30 March), the EUR/USD exchange rate is 1.15. The net assets in the subsidiary can be thought of as PPE that they have purchased, net of any operating liabilities.[7] This corresponds to the equity investment the parent company has made in the subsidiary. Another change in the table is that we now look at currency translation GLs (CTGLs), rather than derivative GLs.

In Panel 1 in Table 6.4 we can see how both the bond and net assets are initially reported at €23 mn. Then the US dollar strengthens, such that both increase by €3 mn due to translation effects. Because of the difference in accounting principles that apply to non-monetary and monetary assets, however, only the loss induced by the higher value of the bond finds its way into net income. The gain from translating the net assets at a stronger dollar will instead go into OCI. While both these accounts are therefore more volatile as a result, it is usually the effect on net income that is a concern to managers. The firm may therefore opt for hedge accounting of the bond, which is shown in Panel 2 in Table 6.4. Now the company is allowed to move the loss on the bond to OCI, leaving a zero impact on net income. Because this loss cancels out the gain on the net assets that was already included in the CTGL, the firm reports zero in OCI as well. The organization has now stabilized equity (by matching the net assets with borrowing in the same currency) but, by using hedge accounting, avoided the undesirable side-effect of more net income volatility.

---

[7] Technically, the parent firm issues a bond and then makes an equity investment in the subsidiary with the proceeds. With the equity injection, the subsidiary purchases the property, plant, and equipment. So, the subsidiary is all equity financed but in the consolidated accounts this equity is eliminated against the shares in the subsidiary that the parent company holds as an asset. We simplify away from these issues to keep the illustration clear.

Table 6.4 Net investment hedge: hedge accounting vs no hedge accounting

Panel 1: No hedge accounting of bond

		20X7.03.30	20X7.06.30
A:	Net assets in subsidiary	23	26
L:	Bond	23	26
E:	Retained earnings	0	−3
E:	Translation reserve	0	3
NI:	FXGL	0	−3
CI:	CTGL	0	3

Panel 2: Hedge accounting of bond

		20X7.03.30	20X7.06.30
A:	Net assets in subsidiary	23	26
L:	Bond	23	26
E:	Retained earnings	0	0
E:	Translation reserve	0	0
NI:	FXGL	0	0
CI:	CTGL	0	0

Requirements for Hedge Accounting

Hedge accounting offers firms a way to reduce unwanted effects on important bottom lines like net income and equity. To qualify for hedge accounting, however, the hedge transaction must meet certain requirements.

The first and most fundamental requirement is that the hedged item is *highly likely* to occur. As a rule of thumb, highly likely means a 90% probability (or higher) of taking place. It is therefore actually possible to hedge an anticipated transaction (that is not yet on the company's books) if it can be argued to be very likely to happen. Such an assessment could be made based on historical patterns. A Swedish firm that has been exporting to Germany for over a decade may be considered highly likely to have receivables in euros also one, two, or three years from now.

The firm also has to provide sufficient documentation to demonstrate that several other requirements have been met, including:

- **Risk management objective.** What is the hedge supposed to achieve?
- **Type of hedge.** Is it a cash flow hedge, fair value hedge, or net investment hedge?
- **Risk exposure being hedged.** Is it interest rate risk, exchange risk, or commodity price risk?
- **The hedged item.** Which item specifically is being hedged (receivable, net investment, etc.)?
- **The hedging instrument.** Details on type of instrument, maturity, counterparty, etc.
- **Hedge effectiveness.** Evidence that the hedge is likely to be effective in reducing the risk related to the hedged item.

Table 6.5 contains an example of documentation for hedge accounting for each of these requirements.

Of these requirements, the one that the majority of managers find the most troublesome to comply with (and understand in the first place!) is proving that the hedge is 'effective'. Hedge

Table 6.5   Hedge accounting requirements according to IFRS 9

Requirement	Documentation
Risk management objective	To protect the value in euros of a US$20 mn receivable against fluctuations in the EUR/USD exchange rate
Type of hedge	Cash flow hedge
Nature of risk being hedged	Foreign exchange risk (the variability in the euro value of the receivable)
Hedging instrument	The forward contract with reference number 012345 with bank XYZ as counterparty
Hedged item	US$20 mn receivable due on 30 September 20X0
Effectiveness (including sources of ineffectiveness)	Prospective test: due to the terms of the hedge and the hedge item matching, the hedge is expected to be highly effective

effectiveness has a very specific meaning in this context. It is defined as follows:

Hedge effectiveness $= \Delta$Fair value of hedge$/\Delta$Fair value of hedged item

This way of calculating hedge effectiveness is referred to as the **dollar offset method**. To illustrate with a simple example, assume that a US-based firm hedges a euro receivable with a forward contract on EUR/USD and opts for hedge accounting. The receivable as well as the hedge have a one-year time horizon. On the next balance sheet date, the firm evaluates the change in fair value of both the receivable and the forward contract. If the receivable is found to have changed in value by US$20 mn and the forward contract by US$21 mn, hedge effectiveness is calculated as 21/20 = 105%.[8] The ineffective part of the derivative's fair value change (i.e. US$1 mn of

---

[8] The value of these two items could develop differently if, for example, the customer's creditworthiness deteriorates, which lowers the value of the commercial transaction due to credit risk.

the total change in value) would be reported in net income, whereas the remaining effective part (i.e. US$20 mn) would be reported in OCI. Observe that the receivable is not *actually* fair value accounted, but the firm is called on to value it *as if it were* for the purpose of determining effectiveness.

In US GAAP, effectiveness must lie between 80% and 125% to qualify for hedge accounting *at all*. If it ends up outside this interval the entire hedge payoff would be considered ineffective and reported in net income. If the value change on the forward contract had been US$27 mn instead, for example, hedge effectiveness would have been 135%, and the hedge would not have qualified. In this case, the full amount (US$27 mn) would be considered ineffective and therefore included in net income. In IFRS 9, the requirement on retrospective hedge effectiveness has been dropped. Instead, firms are supposed to (1) demonstrate an economic relationship between the hedge instrument and the hedge item, (2) show that credit risk does not dominate (i.e. is larger than) the magnitude of this relationship, and (3) indicate that the hedge ratio is held constant over the life of the hedge.

A hedge effectiveness assessment is supposed to recur at each balance sheet date throughout the hedge's life. This is referred to as a 'prospective test', meaning that the firm looks ahead and asks anew whether the hedge is likely to be effective going forward. Often, such an assessment is based on an analysis of historical data up to that point, using the dollar offset method.

Hedge effectiveness is also to be assessed at the inception of the hedge. In this case the dollar offset method is not available since no historical patterns can be observed. The firm can then use one of two approaches: **critical terms matching** or one of several **analytical methods**. Critical terms matching is about checking whether the terms (currency, nominal amount, maturity, etc.) are similar enough so that effectiveness can simply be taken for granted. If the receivable amounts to €100 mn being due in six months, and the forward contract specifies exactly that amount of euros being exchanged in six months, then obviously there is going to be a high degree of correspondence. The analytical methods include simulation and regression analysis techniques, where one builds spreadsheet-based scenarios of how both the hedge and the hedge item perform under different sets of assumptions. The degree to which their payoffs correlate in these scenarios can then be assessed to determine effectiveness.

Some Perspectives on Hedge Accounting

The advantage of hedge accounting is that it offers firms a tool for keeping unrealized GLs from affecting corporate bottom lines until the hedging transaction is actually due. Achieving more stable bottom lines is clearly desirable, all else being equal. But other things are not equal, as we will discuss in detail below.

The first and most obvious drawback of hedge accounting is the cost. The requirement to comply with the requirements, in particular documenting hedge effectiveness on an ongoing basis, can place a significant burden on an organization. Several individuals need to be involved in what is often a time-consuming activity that demands skills in advanced accounting and valuation issues. Firms that choose not to use hedge accounting indeed cite the costs of documentation and compliance as the number one reason for their decision.

But increasing costs is not the only drawback of hedge accounting. It also impacts the transparency of financial reports in a negative way. This might seem like an unfair accusation at first, given that the purpose is usually to keep the firm's net income tidy and clean. But anyone who has browsed through the annual report of a firm that uses hedge accounting understands this point. These reports tend to be full of esoteric jargon and technicalities related to hedge accounting. There is a massive assault on the reader as the firm tries to show that it complies with the relevant standards and is doing hedge accounting 'by the book'. The end result, unfortunately, is near-incomprehensible clutter, beyond the ability of most people who are not hedge accountants by profession. The amount of information increases, but transparency decreases.

These are serious concerns in our view, so hedge accounting should not be adopted lightly. One must also ask why firms are so afraid of unrealized GLs in net income anyway. If the answer is that the stock price will become more volatile as a consequence, then one is assuming that market participants are unable to implement simple analytical adjustments. As discussed in Chapter 1, in business schools around the world students are taught to adjust away performance effects that are temporary and/or financial when valuing a firm's core business. Unrealized GLs related to derivatives are most definitely part of the items taken out of the forecasts of cash flow. Financial analysts are indeed known to have a rock-hard focus on operating performance. In our experience, just as with translation effects on monetary ALs, unrealized GLs related to FX derivatives often seem to pass them by without hardly being noticed. If so, then firms need not worry about such GLs being cap-italized into the stock price. For that to happen, investors must be using very simplistic P/E multiples that do not distinguish between short-term noise and the sustainable operating performance of the core business.

The notion that investors capitalize unrealized GLs, leading to excess volatility in the stock price, is especially peculiar given that the same GL is disclosed even if the firm applies hedge account-ing. In fact, it is reported just a bit further down on the same page. Remember that all hedge accounting does is to move the unreal-ized GL from net income to OCI. Well, OCI is shown just below the net income statement! How can it be that supposedly sophisticated investors treat a GL differently if it is shown in net income or other comprehensive income when the two are sitting right next to each other in the financial report? It would take a monumental glitch in their analytical capabilities for that to happen.

In some industries, analysts seem to consider net income hardly relevant at all. In the oil and gas industry, for example, analysts mainly worry about key operating indicators like the replacement ratio and the break-even cost of production. These are core value drivers that speak volumes about the future cash-flow-generating ability of the firm. Net income as a measure of performance is not high on that list. Under such circumstances, hedge accounting appears to have a fairly weak case: why spend resources protecting something that few can be bothered to pay a lot of attention to anyway?

In other contexts, however, the focus on net income may be stronger. Especially in industries where clear operating performance measures are lacking that could easily take its place. Perhaps the firm has observed that, in the past, the stock market has reacted excessively to earnings 'surprises' in its industry. It is not implausible that the stock market views stable earnings as a modest positive, associating few surprises with good management.[9] Given the pride of place of net income as a shorthand for communicating performance in the business world, it is understandable that there is a general preference for not letting it become too volatile. The more weight management puts on these aspects, the stronger the case in favour of hedge accounting.

Key Chapter Takeaways

> Derivatives are fair value accounted, meaning that they are shown in the balance sheet at their fair market value.
> A mismatch occurs because the commercial transaction being hedged (i.e. an anticipated cash flow) is not fair value accounted.
> Because of this mismatch, net income may in fact become more, not less, volatile because changes in fair value have to be reported as gains or losses.
> Hedge accounting is the solution on offer to avoid the consequences of this mismatch. It allows firms to report the fair value gains or losses in other comprehensive income rather than net income.

---

[9] In financial theory, earnings volatility is not a priced factor and the claim seems generally disputed by academic finance, which tends to view it as a myth that accounting choices influence value. Among practitioners, however, the claim that a stable net income is valuable and 'good' is often heard.

➤ The accumulated fair value gains or losses are 'stored' in an equity account called the hedging reserve until the hedging contract matures, when they are 'released back' into net income as a realized gain or loss.
➤ While solving the problem of 'paper volatility' arising from fair value accounting, hedge accounting comes with substantial costs.
➤ Chief among these costs are the requirements to document hedge effectiveness on an ongoing basis, and the reduced comprehensibility of financial reports.

Further Reading

Ramirez, J. 2015. *Accounting for Derivatives: Advanced Hedging under IFRS*. Wiley: Hoboken, NJ.

Chapter 7
Centralizing Exposure Management

Derivatives, on paper, seem to be an almost ideal tool for managing a firm's risk–return profile. In the previous chapter we brought attention to one of the real-world factors that limit their popularity in practice, namely the fact that they are fair value accounted when business transactions are not. Here, we address another factor that complicates the existence of derivatives in firms. There are, it turns out, many units within a corporate group with their own view on how FX risk should be managed.

The background for this chapter is the seemingly legitimate request of business units to get access to FX derivatives so that they can manage *their* risk. After all, they are responsible for their own performance and evaluated on their ability to improve it. Often these performance measures are heavily exposed to exchange rate risk. Is it not reasonable, then, that they get access to financial derivatives to manage that risk and protect their performance? FX derivative usage thus comes attached with a management control issue: shall business units be allowed to use FX derivatives, and if so, what rules should guide this activity?

These questions are related to the broader question of *who* should be responsible for FXRM (of which derivative usage is part). Studies have shown that the managerial factor in risk management is a big one. Contrary to what is assumed in academic theories targeting value maximization, the incentives and preferences of the decision-makers are highly influential on decisions involving risk.

In this chapter, we argue that a corporate group should pursue a largely centralized approach to FXRM (i.e. one that leaves little scope for business units to set their hedge ratios independently and/or carry out hedging transactions with banks). A centralized FXRM also implies that financing and capital structure policy (including the currency composition of debt) is determined by headquarters, not in the business units. The advantages of a centralized form of FXRM are simply too great to ignore. Centralized FXRM does not have to imply, however, that business units have to 'unfairly' accept large exposures to FX. We will discuss various ways this 'risk management gap' at the business unit level can be closed.

Centralized FX Hedging Defined

To keep the exposition simple, we focus our discussion on the centralization of the FX hedging decision (i.e. the use of financial derivatives at the corporate vs business unit level). An analogous analysis can be done regarding the management of currency composition of the firm's assets and liabilities (debt and cash in particular). We return to that issue, and a broader FXRM perspective, at the end of the chapter.

In this chapter, we use the terms 'headquarters' and 'central' loosely. Centralized decision-making does not mean one thing. A risk management function may also weigh in on FX hedging policy. In the remainder of the chapter, we refer, for simplicity, simply to 'headquarters' as the relevant unit in centralized FXRM.

The question of how, and by whom, FXRM decisions are to be made more specifically is saved for Chapters 8 and 9.

We start by addressing the fundamental question of what it means to manage FX hedging centrally. Many associate centralized FX hedging with headquarters' control over external transactions. That is, no-one but a central function in headquarters can enter derivative contracts with banks or other market-makers. But this definition neglects something equally important, which is the question of who gets to decide FX hedging policy. Full centralization occurs when the firm has centralized control over FX transactions *and* the FX hedging policy.

The interaction between the transaction and policy dimensions of FXRM is illustrated in Table 7.1. The approach is fully decentralized if business areas hedge according to their own wishes and deal directly with banks (upper left). Partial centralization is at hand if headquarters control transactions but not policy, or if they control policy but not transactions. Full centralization requires both transactions and policy to be handled by headquarters.

A look at actual practice quickly reveals that the way FX hedging is organized varies greatly. For example, ABB, a Swiss-based power and automation company, states in its annual report that its subsidiaries are 'required by company policy to hedge binding sales'. Trelleborg, a Swedish polymer technology company, states that 'a portion of the ... net exposure is hedged by Group Treasury based on the business areas' hedging decisions'. Ratos, in contrast, a diversified investment company, writes that currency risk in its

Table 7.1 Centralized vs decentralized FXRM

FX policy		FX derivative transactions	
		Business units	Headquarters
	Business units	Decentralization	Partial centralization
	Headquarters	Partial centralization	Centralization

subsidiaries is 'hedged according to the policy of each individual subsidiary'.[1]

Centralization is the norm, however, and an ongoing process in most firms. In a study from 2015 by one of the authors of this book (Jankensgård), it was found that the majority of firms in a broad sample of Swedish-listed firms that were identified as FX derivative users have centralized FXRM. A sizeable minority, however, fail to centralize in at least one of the two dimensions (23% of all derivative users). In most cases, decentralization was a result of allowing business areas some degree of influence on the hedging policy. The cases in which headquarters set the policy but business units execute it externally hardly exist. The cases in which headquarters do all the external transactions but where units can influence policy, however, are quite common.

Benefits of Centralization

Various advantages of centralized hedging have been identified in the literature. These fall into two categories, one related to the centralization of transactions and the other of policy. Here, we list those related to the centralized handling of transactions:

- **Hedging net rather than gross exposures.** When each business unit hedges its exposure, a firm may fail to recognize that some of its exposures net out naturally. If one unit purchases in US dollars while at the same time another unit sells in US dollars, then hedging both exposures is inefficient since from the company's perspective they cancel each other out. By centralizing transactions, central staff can net revenues and costs in the same currency and go external only with the net exposure.
- **Achieve better terms from banks.** If headquarters pool (and net) the exposures to be hedged, they can negotiate better terms (i.e. a lower bid–ask spread) with the bank than each business unit could individually.

---

[1] All information taken from annual reports from 2015.

- **Lower costs.** If business units execute their derivatives externally, each unit must have its own staff and systems to administer these transactions. By centralizing, this layer of administrative resources can be eliminated.
- **Build-up of expertise.** By pooling its resources and competence centrally, a company develops the necessary expertise to manage the various aspects of currency risk, and to act as qualified decision support to senior management in currency-related issues.
- **Better control over risks.** When more people are allowed to handle currency derivatives throughout the organization, the larger is the risk that something goes wrong, either by mishandling or by rogue speculation in currencies. By restricting access to derivatives to headquarters, this risk is mitigated.

To these benefits we should add those that result from centralization of FX hedging policy:

- **Focus on operational as opposed to financial matters.** By requiring business units to follow a company policy, they do not have to spend time developing a hedging policy of their own. Rather, business units can focus their energies on what they do best, which is running their business operations.
- **Less opportunistic behaviour.** Left to their own devices, business units may be tempted to take views on the future direction of exchange rates and adjust hedging strategies in an attempt to make money from outsmarting the market. With a centralized policy in place this behaviour is curbed, with more consistent hedging over time as a result.
- **Balance in company positions.** If business units are free to set their own hedge ratios, some units may choose to hedge and others not. This could lead to an imbalance in the currency positions of the company as a whole, or actually increase risk in some circumstances.
- **Coordination of FX hedging with other policies.** Various corporate policies need to be coordinated in an effort to manage the firm's total risk–return profile. Hedging can be integrated more successfully into such a framework if it is centralized first.

Of these, which are the most important? Among the transaction-related benefits the respondents in the study by Jankensgård cited 'increased control' as the most important, closely followed by 'better rates'. Among the policy-related benefits, most respondents claimed 'improved focus on operations' as the main benefit. To summarize, firms centralize FX hedging chiefly to increase control over the flow of transactions, lower the cost of hedging, and make sure business units focus on the right things.

Decentralization is not completely without merits, however. In some cases, respondents argued that the quality of forecasts obtained from business units will be higher if there is a sense of ownership by the units, which can only happen if they are allowed to manage their own exposures. More vaguely, some also stated that business units 'are closer to the action and know best', for example when forecasts are uncertain and need to be continually fine-tuned in order not to end up with too much or too little hedging. On the whole, though, we maintain that such claims are a long shot from standing up to the impressive case in favour of centralization.

Why do so many firms still fail to centralize despite the overwhelming benefits? Many respondents said that decentralized FXRM 'hangs together' with a decentralized business model. In these firms, the business units operate quite independently of the parent company and may even have responsibility for their own capital structure. In that context, centralizing the hedging decision may be somewhat out of tune with the general company philosophy. Obviously, these firms are choosing to say no to some of the benefits that are normally seen as the low-hanging fruits of having a corporate group, namely to centralize corporate functions like financing and risk management.

A more sinister explanation for the lack of centralization is that it is the result of a 'power grab' by independent-minded business unit managers who cherish their autonomy. In these companies, the balance of power between the units and headquarters is such that the latter cannot easily implement a centralized approach. This line of explanation was suggested by several of the respondents in the study by Jankensgård.

Internal Hedging Arrangements

Where does implementing a centralized approach leave business units' legitimate desire to protect and manage their own performance with regard to FX? Some companies may choose to deal with this issue by creating an internal hedging arrangement. The idea with internal hedging is that headquarters is the counterparty to the hedge rather than a bank. Headquarters' control over derivative transactions is thereby ensured because they can net all the internal hedges and hedge externally only the amounts that are desirable from a corporate point of view. The goal of hedging net rather than gross exposures is therefore also facilitated.

The basic idea behind an internal hedging arrangement is illustrated in Figure 7.1. The various internal hedges are netted out against each other, and headquarters only go external with the net amount in US dollars (the euro exposure cancels out altogether). There is thus a significant reduction in the number of external contracts compared to the situation where business units hedge directly with banks.

Few will argue against the benefits of concentrating bank contracts to headquarters so that the company can enjoy better rates and other benefits from a strategic, long-term relationship with the bank

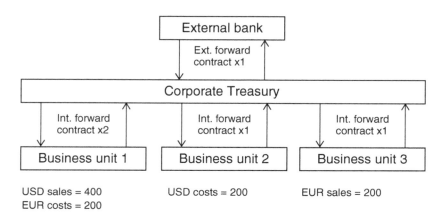

Figure 7.1 Internal vs external hedge

in question. An internal hedging system is a practical way of achieving these benefits for firms that consider it reasonable for business units to have access to derivatives.

Our recommended approach, however, would also involve giving little or no discretion to business units in terms of deciding their own hedging policy. This advice runs contrary to how the merits of internal hedging arrangements are sometimes presented. In the standard approach, business units are free to hedge as they see fit with headquarters as counterparty. Then, headquarters basically ignores these contracts and instead makes an external hedge based on its own policy and forecasted net exposures. This seemingly combines the benefits of keeping the external hedging decision firmly in headquarters with the added bonus of allowing business units to manage their own exposures as they think best. Thanks to internal hedging it might seem that everyone is going to be happy.

There are, however, certain problems with giving business areas freedom to hedge even within an internal hedging arrangement. Several of the disadvantages we discussed earlier will start creeping back. First of all, it keeps business units spending their energies on FX hedging, for which there is little rationale from a corporate point of view. Second, FXRM business units, as well as headquarters, need to maintain an administration of FX transactions, which is a cost element for the firm. Third, any internal contract that is not mirrored by an external one is likely to be met with suspicion by business units. If it is not a real external contract then it is just 'Mickey Mouse money', so what is the point? Fourth, the gains and losses related to internal derivatives affect separate legal entities with their own taxable income and capital structure. While from the company's perspective the payoffs cancel out, they may still impact liquidity and taxes paid in each group company in potentially suboptimal ways.

A final point to consider is that allowing firms to hedge freely with internal contracts means that the GLs on these FX derivatives will end up in these units' net financial expenses, which is a line below EBIT. This would appear to suggest that these units would have to be evaluated on net income for the internal contracts to have a meaningful impact on their performance. Using net income as performance metric in turn would seem to necessitate handing over to the units the responsibility for managing their capital structure too, so that they can influence the entirety of their financial expenses. All of which, unfortunately, runs contrary to the idea of centralization of FXRM and all the previously mentioned benefits.

The takeaway from this discussion is that central control over hedging policy (i.e. when and how much to hedge) must be assured even when an internal hedging arrangement is in place. We know of companies that hedge externally what they believe to be the correct amounts for the firm, given their net exposures, and then 'allocate' all these hedges to their business areas through internal hedge contracts. There is then no residual exposure in the parent company, and headquarters can take tax and liquidity effects in different business units into account when needed.

To achieve the goal of central control over hedging policy, other firms may choose to dictate a specific hedging policy that the business units are then expected to follow, for example, in terms of setting a target hedge ratio.

Business units may of course resent the loss of agency that results from centralizing FXRM along these lines. One might suspect, however, that any discontent resulting from a push towards centralization is likely to be short-lived. Perhaps the units even come to see the advantages of a centralized approach. Whereas before they may have been blamed if a certain hedging strategy ended up badly, now they can just point to the central policy, whatever the outcome. And a lack of opportunities to hedge independently is only a problem if the business unit would have hedged significantly differently than the policy set by headquarters.

Dealing with FX Exposures in Business Units

Rather than implement a potentially cumbersome internal hedging arrangement, firms may try to make FX a non-issue in business units. Companies can and do pursue other ways of reducing currency exposures. The units' interest in FX derivatives can be lowered drastically if the performance evaluation system is designed to make currency fluctuations irrelevant to managers. Consider as an example Boliden, a Swedish-listed company in the mining industry. Its business units have been integrated in the group for a long period and, in terms of rewarding its business unit managers, financial performance measures have to a large extent been replaced by operational ones. For these reasons, FX is of little concern to the managers on a decentralized level. Another case in point is the retail industry. In retailers the parent company, which is usually also the production unit, sells the goods to its selling units in their own functional currency. Since the revenues of the units tend to be generated exclusively in the home market, they are perfectly 'unexposed' and obtain a balance sheet free from currency effects. Any currency exposure ends up entirely with the parent company.

The general idea is to give monetary performance measures like EBIT and net income less weight in the performance evaluation that forms the basis of variable pay. Instead, firms should seek to gradually increase the weight on other key performance indicators (KPIs) that are largely free of currency effects (whilst also connected to value creation!).

A more radical option should also be on the table: simply disallow business units the ability to use derivatives once and for all. In this case, the units are expected to simply live with, and accept, any impact on their performance from changes in exchange rates. Some respondents in the study by Jankensgård had done this, citing, among other things, a desire to have the units respond to the changing realities dynamically and not 'hide' behind derivatives. That is, pricing and production strategies would be more quickly adjusted if the units immediately feel the effect of changes in exchange rates. The philosophy in these companies seems to be that changing conditions, including exchange rates, are a fact of business life and we had better face up to them.

A dilemma that one encounters when centralizing FXRM is that business units, when freed of their responsibilities to manage FX actively, lack incentives to produce good forecasts of FX exposures. Headquarters can counteract any such tendency to lose interest by making high-quality forecasts part of the KPIs that are linked to the unit managers' yearly compensation. Another issue is that business units need to remain competent in FX issues to correctly understand the pricing of commercial deals. Product prices may be quoted in different currencies, and a solid understanding throughout the organization of how this works is necessary to ensure the best deals are obtained. Even with centralized FXRM, business units must maintain sufficient understanding of how their commercial activities relate to exchange rates and do their part in making sure central decision-makers have a good overview of commercial exposures. For this purpose, headquarters must be vigilant in ensuring that this competence is maintained (e.g. by in-house training) and that there are clear lines of communication between the business units and headquarters.

The Centralization Process

Centralization is an ongoing process in many firms. While most firms are striving to centralize to a higher degree, it may not be possible to implement a fully centralized approach overnight. Whenever another firm is acquired and consolidated into the group, managers face the task of somehow integrating the FXRM of the acquired firm into the corporate fold. In some firms this may be a quick and efficient process, whereas in others the acquired firm can live on like a quasi-independent unit for many years, hanging on to its old FXRM policy.

Complete centralization may not even be desirable for all firms. As noted already, a highly decentralized business model may be viewed as incompatible with a fully centralized version of FXRM. Business unit independence can furthermore be partial and co-exist with a largely centralized approach. For example, the corporate policy may stipulate that hedging should be within a certain interval, say 40–60% of a given exposure, but leave units to decide on the exact hedge ratio. Business units may also be expected to follow a corporate policy but be allowed to present a 'hedging case' in rare circumstances, say a large investment project, that sidesteps the corporate policy.

Allowing some scope for decentralized influence on decision-making may occasionally be warranted, but it is a slippery slope. What must be avoided is a situation where a steady stream of hedging proposals from various business units and projects are dealt with on an ad-hoc basis. In such firms, hedging becomes erratic and unpredictable, and time and energy are unnecessarily spent on FX hedging discussions. Decentralized influence on the firm's external hedging should be kept to a minimum. Headquarters should strive to have a unified and streamlined approach to FXRM, which can then be managed with an eye to the firm's overall risk–return profile.

Key Chapter Takeaways

➢ An important question in FXRM is at which organizational level foreign exchange risk is managed.

➢ FXRM can be managed at a decentralized level (by business units) or at a centralized level (by headquarters).

➢ Centralization of FXRM has two dimensions: who is responsible for transactions with banks, and who gets to decide FX policy. Complete centralization requires both dimensions to be concentrated to headquarters.

➢ Centralization of transactions has benefits in terms of facilitating netting; obtaining lower transaction costs; and improving control.

➢ Centralization of FX policy has benefits in terms of reducing a layer of administration; getting business units to focus on improving operations; and facilitating the integration of FX policies with other corporate policies.

➤ The conundrum is that business units may feel they have a legitimate claim on tools for managing FX exposures that affect the performance measures they are evaluated on. This can be addressed with internal hedging arrangements, or by shifting performance evaluation towards operating KPIs.

➤ Companies are recommended to pursue a high degree of centralization, whilst preserving enough competence in business units in FX-related issues to understand pricing of commercial deals and ensure high-quality exposure forecasts.

Further Reading

Belk, P. A. 2002. The organization of foreign exchange management: A three-country study. *Managerial Finance* **28**, 43–53.

Jankensgård, H. 2015. Does centralisation of FX derivative usage impact firm value? *European Financial Management* **21**, 309–332.

Chapter 8
Integrated Risk Management

O ne of the most important trends in corporate risk management is the rise of integrated approaches to managing risk, such as the increasingly popular enterprise risk management (ERM). Centralizing FXRM is not enough for integrated risk management (IRM) to happen, however. It is quite possible to have a fully centralized control over FX transactions and FX policy yet still qualify as the opposite of IRM: 'silo-based' risk management. Silos refer to risk management activities carried out independently of other efforts to manage risk in the firm.

In fact, FXRM is often viewed as a classic risk management silo. Historically, it has been the domain of the treasury department, whose recommendations have tended to be merely 'rubber-stamped' by the board of directors. In some firms, there are even silos *within* the FX silo. These are cases where treasury's efforts to manage various facets of FXRM are fragmented rather than coordinated.

Adopting IRM has important implications for FXRM. IRM, in many ways, challenges the traditional role of the treasury and its handling of FXRM within the company. Proponents of IRM tend to view the firm's board of directors, the supposed guardians of the best interest of shareholders, as the ultimate 'owner' of the firm's risk profile. The board does not run the firm on a day-to-day basis, however, so a body analysing risk management decisions on their behalf is needed to implement IRM. The so-called risk committee is just such a forum, where risk management policies are debated from the viewpoint of the firm as a whole.

The essence of FXRM as part of an integrated effort to manage risk is that FX policy is shifted from the treasury department to a risk committee that focuses on the firm's total risk–return profile. In this approach, FXRM policy is set so as to help ensure that various corporate-level performance thresholds are not threatened, such as being able to implement the business plan, or meeting debt covenants, while maintaining an adequate upside potential. Treasury, of course, given its technical competence in FXRM, will be an important contributor to such a risk committee.

Silo-Based Risk Management

To understand the rise of IRM, it helps to get a clear picture of what came before it. IRM proponents usually contrast it with 'silo-based' risk management. A silo should here be taken to mean something that stands in isolation, not integrated with the rest. A firm typically has a considerable number of risk exposures that arise as a consequence of doing business (some of which are illustrated in Figure 8.1). The silo approach implies that each is assessed and managed on a stand-alone basis. Because of the fragmentation, exposures are not netted in this approach, and there is little coordination of risk mitigation efforts. Methodologies for managing risk can be very different in the various departments, as can the terminology surrounding it. There is, as a consequence, no unified 'risk language'.

FXRM is often used as an illustration of silo risk management. Traditionally, it has been carried out by treasury (or the finance department, depending on how the firm is organized; we will use

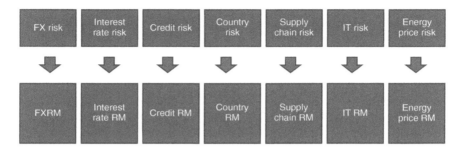

Figure 8.1   Examples of risk management silos

'treasury' as shorthand). Even though the FX hedging policy is ultimately endorsed by the board of directors, it is often seen as merely 'rubber-stamping' what the treasury proposes. The real powers regarding which exposures are hedged and which are not have to a significant degree been invested in the treasury. What is more, the treasury in many companies has also enjoyed a certain freedom to take views on exchange rates. In these firms, using the treasury's expertise regarding currencies and interest rates in this way is seen as a natural part of minimizing the cost of financing.

FXRM in many companies therefore meets the definition of a silo: policies are set without regard to other risk exposures in the firm, using localized jargon and definitions of exposures. There may even be silos *within* the FX silo (as depicted in Figure 8.2). There are numerous ways an FX exposure can be framed, and therefore many possibilities for different FX exposures to be managed in ways that are not completely integrated with one another. One activity may concern the hedging of exposures related to receivables or payables ('trade'). Another group of people may be concerned with reducing volatility in net income. Others may be pursuing FX derivatives in an attempt to beat the market. Yet others may be specifically concerned with translation GLs on one or more subsidiaries. Sometimes there is a strong focus on FX effects on liquidity, including the translation of cash held by foreign subsidiaries.

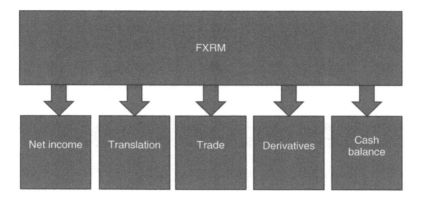

Figure 8.2   FXRM silos

The Core Principles of IRM

What is IRM? IRM is a lot of things, and different people will offer different definitions of it, but it rests on a few core principles. We can glean some insights about these principles from portfolio theory, which has been studied by researchers in finance since the intellectual breakthrough of Henry Markowitz in 1952. Portfolio theory eventually earned Markowitz a Nobel Prize in economics, and continues to be the intellectual bedrock for risk management. The word portfolio, in this context, refers to a group of assets brought together and viewed on the basis of their joint performance and risk. While Markowitz had in mind a portfolio of financial securities, such as stocks and bonds, we can view the firm as a portfolio of cash-flow-generating business units and explore the analogy.

In portfolio theory, investors, who are risk-averse, optimize their expected return for any given level of risk. How can they do this? Key to understanding portfolio behaviour is the role of correlations. A correlation is a statistical measure of how much two variables, such as the return on two different assets, tend to move together. More formally, it is a measure of the strength and direction of a linear relationship between two variables. The correlation coefficient can range between −1 and 1, where positive values indicate that the variables, on average, move in the same direction. Negative correlations, in contrast, imply that the variables tend to move in opposite directions (i.e. when one goes up the other is more likely to go down, and vice versa).

The magic of correlations lies in what happens when more securities are added to the portfolio. It turns out that the expected return on the portfolio remains a weighted average of the individual assets no matter how many they are. The risk of the portfolio, however, does not, on condition that correlations are not perfect and positive (=1). Here, risk is understood as variance, which is a measure of the degree of dispersion around the expected outcome. When more securities are added, the variance of the portfolio is *less* than the weighted average of the variance of the individual assets. This is the risk-reducing effect of **diversification**, a modern-day word for the age-old wisdom of not putting all one's eggs in the same basket. It is by making use of correlations that one can combine securities into portfolios in ways that are more 'efficient', in the sense that they offer more expected return for a given level of risk.

This very brief recap of portfolio theory establishes two of the basic tenets of IRM. The first is that it is the risk–return characteristics of the portfolio that matter, not the individual units. The second is that the correlation between the units in the portfolio has a potentially large influence on overall risk.

An interesting special case is when the correlation is negative and perfect. For a financial investor a correlation of −1 does not normally happen. It can be thought of as a situation where the owner of the portfolio is simultaneously long *and* short in the same asset and where the positions exactly offset each other.[1] It is like shorting a stock and holding it at the same time. For investors in financial markets this is not an attractive proposition, as it implies transaction costs but no potential for gain. For firms, however, such

---

[1] A long position refers to a positive net exposure (i.e. when the firm benefits from an *increase* in the price (or rate), for example an exporter generating sales in a foreign currency). A short position refers to a negative net exposure (i.e. when the firm benefits from a *decrease* in the price or rate).

a situation often arises naturally, not least with respect to exchange rates. The simplest and most frequently occurring example is when firms buy and sell in the same currency, creating both long and short positions at the same time. For multinational firms, this is the rule rather than the exception.

The case of buying and selling in the same currency hints at some limitations in the analogy between a portfolio of financial assets and a corporate group. Because what really does a corporate 'portfolio' consist of? Earlier we suggested that the answer is the business units that make up the corporate group. But business units, whether they are organized as divisions, business areas, or subsidiaries, are often highly complex in their own right, with multiple exposures to different risks like exchange rates, energy prices, and credit risks.

The observation that business units have multiple exposures, often to the same risk factors, indicates another possible take on portfolio theory as applied to the firm. From a risk management perspective, we could alternatively think of a company in terms of a portfolio of exposures to different risk factors, ignoring the question of which organizational unit they originate in. A risk factor is here defined as a stochastic (uncertain) variable whose outcome impacts corporate performance. An exchange rate is certainly a risk factor according to this definition.

We have now arrived at a third principle of IRM in firms: exposures must be addressed on a net, rather than a gross, basis. To know the final exposure to any given risk factor we must, on a firm-wide basis, subtract short positions from long positions in that risk factor. For exchange rates, this corresponds to the straightforward principle of netting exposures discussed in Chapter 2. 'Natural hedges', which is to say offsetting exposures, may exist in different parts of the organization. From the perspective of the corporate group, only the net number is relevant.

We are now ready to summarize the three cornerstones of IRM:

1. Risk and return are analysed from the perspective of the firm as a whole, not from the units that it consists of.

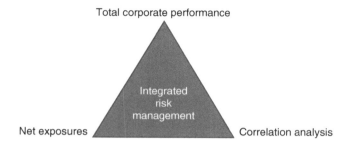

Figure 8.3   Core elements of integrated risk management

2. Exposures to risk factors are identified and assessed on a net basis rather than gross.
3. Correlations between risk factors are utilized to understand overall risk.

Figure 8.3 sums up the elements of IRM. Each of the different parts is described in more detail in the remainder of this chapter.

Netting Exposures

The idea behind netting is of course simple: just deduct your costs in one currency from your revenue in that currency. We have discussed some of the practical challenges in accomplishing netting in practice: the sheer complexity of modern multinationals; low-quality forecasts; inconsistent definitions of exposures; and shortcomings of internal systems for data aggregation all combine to make netting of exposures easier said than done (Chapter 2). We have added another complicating factor, namely that FXRM in some firms is decentralized (Chapter 7). When business units set their FX policy independently and handle the related transactions, achieving a meaningful netting of exposures will be all the more difficult. Understanding how FX impacts various facets of corporate performance due to translation effects adds another layer of complexity (Chapters 3 and 4).

The best way to deal with the challenges posed by the complexities of corporate exposures, in our view, is to develop an IRM decision-support tool that explicitly incorporates the exposure dimension. Our own intuitive grasp and back-of-the-envelope calculations usually fall short. It does not take a very large firm or a particularly large number of exposed elements for the complexity to overwhelm the individual.

IRM also calls for going beyond a simple income-statement view of exposures. Firms operate with many indicators of performance, all of which will be exposed differently. For example, capital expenditure (capex) could be largely in foreign currency. These exposures fall outside of the income statement. Yet one of the key motivations for risk management is avoiding situations where the company's cash flows fall below the level needed to service its cash commitments, which includes capex. This suggests that firms also have an interest in measuring exposures on the level of cash flow vs cash commitments. Simultaneously keeping track of exposures at so many different levels of performance requires a well-designed model.

We also advocate that such a decision-support tool accurately reflects translation exposures. The model ideally should be 'IFRS-consistent' or 'US GAAP-consistent', in that the financial statements modelled in it should respond to changes in assumptions about exchange rates in much the same way that the firm's actual financial reports would. Key to this is making use of the OCI and the translation/hedging reserves to make the model's balance sheet 'self-balancing' (i.e. it follows actual accounting principles to reconcile the in- and outgoing balance sheets). Then there is no need for a 'plug' to capture any unspecified and unexplained deviations in the model. This feature greatly increases the confidence one can have in the model's outputs because everything hangs together from an accounting point of view, regardless of which scenario is assumed.

Hydro, a Norwegian aluminium producer, is an example of a company that has undertaken such a modelling effort. It went from a situation with a fragmented approach to FXRM – in which several models existed dealing with different aspects of FX exposure – to having one unified decision-support tool. Apart from a comprehensive modelling of commercial exposures, the model contains a description of the firm's net asset position, the FX exposure matrix, and cash flow exposures to FX on various levels (e.g. the currency composition of capex). All of these things are connected to each other by applying actual accounting principles, rendering consistent forecasts of the firm's financial statements for any set of assumptions about exchange rates (and other risk factors). The model makes it possible to analyse net exposures for the company as a whole, for multiple measures of corporate performance.

Correlation Analysis

Once exposures are on a net basis, we can proceed and analyse the way the risk factors involved tend to move together, or their degree of correlation. In what follows it is important to see that in FXRM one always has to choose a currency to serve as home currency in the analysis. This will usually be the functional currency of the corporate group (i.e. the one it uses to prepare its consolidated financial statements). In this book, as mentioned already, an exchange rate is always expressed in terms of units of home currency per one unit of foreign currency. According to this structure, a Belgian firm would define exposure in terms of its performance measured in euros and use foreign currency/EUR in the analysis of FX exposure.

A positive correlation between the exchange rates tends to arise naturally when a certain home currency is used to measure performance and for quoting exchange rates. This is because, when the home currency weakens, it tends to do so across the board, against all foreign currencies. Perhaps investors worry about that country's expected inflation or political stability, which will reduce the attractiveness of holding the currency on a very general level, leading to a broad depreciation. The Brexit turmoil illustrates this point. As the uncertainty regarding the British economy escalated, the pound was implicated and lost in value vs most other currencies throughout 2016 and 2017.

Exchange rates may also correlate because two foreign currencies tend to move in sync. This could be the case if the two economies are closely interlinked because of extensive trade. The US and Canadian economies, for example, are highly integrated and therefore tend to share the same ups and downs. In some cases, central banks even peg their country's currency to another, thereby creating a close relationship. The Danish krone, for example, has been pegged to the euro via the European Union's exchange rate mechanism, and therefore does not float freely.

Table 8.1 shows correlation coefficients between a set of randomly selected exchange rates for two different home currencies: the US dollar and the Norwegian krone. The purpose is to illustrate how correlations between exchange rates depend on the choice of home currency. The correlations are estimated based on the change in the monthly exchange rates between January 2000 and April 2019. As can be seen in Table 8.1, there is a clear home-currency effect. Nearly all correlations are positive because of the general tendency for the home currency to strengthen or weaken simultaneously vs all other currencies. The 'synched economies' effect is also there. For example, from the viewpoint of a US firm there is a high correlation between SEK/USD and EUR/USD (0.86). Most likely this comes about as a result of the high degree of integration of the Swedish economy into the euro-area. From the vantage point of a Norwegian firm, however, there is a high correlation between CAD/NOK and USD/NOK (0.69, not shown in the table) because the US and Canadian economies are highly interlinked.

Exchange rates may also correlate with other market risks. Most of the world's commodities are priced in US dollars, inducing a natural correlation between that currency and, say, the oil price. In a related way, the exchange rates of major commodity-producing countries also tend to be influenced by price fluctuations in these commodities. A case in point is the Norwegian krone vs the US dollar. Norway is an economy dominated by commodities, notably oil. When the oil price is high, the krone tends to strengthen because the

Table 8.1 Correlation coefficients between exchange rates

Panel 1: Home currency US dollar

	AUD/USD	GBP/USD	YEN/USD	SEK/USD	CAD/USD	MXN/USD	EUR/USD
AUD/USD	1						
GBP/USD	0.500	1					
YEN/USD	0.109	0.147	1				
SEK/USD	0.700	0.664	0.213	1			
CAD/USD	0.696	0.464	0.064	0.597	1		
MXN/USD	0.005	−0.02	0.003	0.013	−0.019	1	
EUR/USD	0.601	0.696	0.278	0.861	0.507	0.003	1

Panel 2: Home currency Norwegian krone

	AUD/NOK	GBP/NOK	YEN/NOK	SEK/NOK	CAD/NOK	MXN/NOK	EUR/NOK
AUD/NOK	1						
GBP/NOK	0.315	1					
YEN/NOK	0.244	0.379	1				
SEK/NOK	0.443	0.450	0.265	1			
CAD/NOK	0.580	0.501	0.433	0.358	1		
MXN/NOK	0.027	0.012	0.034	0.039	0.029	1	
EUR/NOK	0.304	0.556	0.433	0.641	0.336	0.031	1

export of oil generates more dollar sales that need to be converted back to home currency. A high oil price will therefore coincide with a weaker US dollar (in krone terms). As a result, the volatility of the oil price measured in Norwegian krone is much less than one would be led to think by looking at either the oil price or USD/NOK alone.

Exchange rates are also naturally correlated with interest rates. The interest rate determines how attractive it is to hold interest-bearing assets in that currency. Investors, in their search for yield, will gravitate towards the currencies that offer the highest interest rates. An unmatched increase in the interest rate in one country often triggers an increase in the demand for that currency, as investors require it in order to purchase the interest-bearing instruments.

The effect of correlations depends on whether the firm is 'long' or 'short' the exchange rates in question. If the firm has two long positions (net exports in both currencies) it gets the most risk reduction from a low or even negative correlation. What is lost on one is gained on the other. To exemplify, a US firm that exports to both Mexico and Japan has a lower risk because of the weak correlation between these two exchange rates (0.003 in Table 8.1). If it loses on one exchange rate there is no particular tendency for it to also lose on the other. If one exposure is long and the other short (net exports in one currency but net imports in the other), the risk reduction is largest when the correlation is high and positive. A US exporter that exports to the euro-area but buys some of its materials from Sweden experiences a large risk reduction because of the high correlation between these exchange rates (0.86). Whenever the Swedish krona strengthens, making its imports more expensive, the firm benefits from the also stronger euro on its sales side.

Correlations are an important input to risk management programmes, but they are not without caveats. One limitation is that they impose an assumption of a linear relationship. As an approximation of the 'real' relationship it may work reasonably most of the time, but such relationships are often found to be non-linear and dynamic in specific episodes. This is sometimes evident for exchange rates, where we have an abundance of examples of currencies that have collapsed and whose value has melted away very rapidly. Up to the point when a currency implodes, exchange rates may behave 'normally', lending the linear assumption some credence, which blinds us to imbalances that are building up. When such an implosion occurs, the correlation can deviate wildly from historical norms.

Correlations are notorious for being somewhat unstable, even in more normal circumstances. A correlation analysis is likely to give different answers depending on the length of the time period, data resolution, and variable transformation. Particularly for shorter frequencies, such as daily or even intra-daily, correlations are often unstable, and may even switch signs. One way to deal with this problem is to use longer frequencies such as quarterly averages. In addition to being more stable by cancelling out a lot of noise in the data, such a frequency will also match better with how corporate performance is usually measured and communicated. Correlations can and should also be extensively tested and challenged. One way to test the robustness of correlations is to do so-called 'back-testing' using large amounts of historical data. Also, one may qualitatively and critically assess imbalances in the economy that could derail currently observed correlations in the future.

Total Corporate Performance

The point of the previous section is that FX risk managers should analyse and use key correlations (while being mindful of potential pitfalls) when they design risk management strategies. Let us go back to the case of a Norwegian oil-producing firm generating revenue in US dollars. Such a firm has two major exposures: the commodity price and the USD/NOK exchange rate. In a silo-based approach these two exposures are managed independently of each other. Most likely the policy with respect to the exchange rate is handled by treasury, and the exposure to the oil price by the managers of the oil and gas division. Because of this fragmentation of risk management along organizational lines, IRM may in fact fail to materialize despite the fact that we are talking about just two exposures and a very strong, easy-to-observe correlation. In our experience, failures of this kind happen all too frequently.

Under IRM, drawing on the insights from portfolio theory, such a company should either hedge none of the exposures (thus relying on the correlation to reduce risk) or hedge both exposures (to fix the price in Norwegian krone). Hedging just one of the exposures may in fact *increase* portfolio risk. When the oil price goes down, the company can normally expect a stronger dollar to partly compensate it. But if the USD/NOK has been hedged, this compensating effect does not take place. The hedge may therefore reduce risk from a narrow silo perspective, but increase the overall risk of the firm!

In IRM we have the focus on the total risk–return profile of the firm, as opposed to individual silos or business units. But how can the overall risk of the firm be understood and measured? A useful place to start is the commercial cash flows of the firm. Cash flow is the performance metric to which net exposures are first mapped up, using either a bottom-up approach or a statistical exposure model (as discussed in Chapter 2). The risk-reducing effect of correlations is therefore best demonstrated in terms of its impact on the variability of cash flow. To continue the example, such an analysis would reveal that a stand-alone hedge of the USD/NOK exchange rate in fact only serves to increase cash flow risk. Operating cash flow presents us with a clear metric by which to judge performance and risk on a portfolio basis.

But, as we emphasize in this book, corporate performance is multifaceted. Companies care about cash flow, but they also care about a large number of other performance indicators, such as net income and different financial ratios that are part of their financial management system. In a decision-support tool of the kind referred to above, the modelling of corporate performance is extended to cover these performance indicators as well. As noted, in order to achieve this, the modelling must integrate forecasts of cash flow, the net income statement, and the balance sheet, reflecting relevant accounting rules and hedge accounting procedures (as described in previous chapters). The analysis of the firm's risk profile is further enhanced if we introduce critical threshold levels of performance that imply the breach of a corporate objective, such as the availability of cash flow in relation to cash commitments. We then have an entirely different basis for setting FX risk policy: a connection between assumptions about exchange rates, corporate performance, and critical thresholds that capture key objectives of the firm. How to communicate such links between FX policy and performance to internal decision-makers is further explored in Chapter 10.

IRM Programmes: Beyond the Core Principles

The principles behind IRM are increasingly practiced by firms. When practitioners speak of IRM it is usually ERM they mean. ERM has been defined by Gates (2006) as a 'board-supervised process for integrated risk management'. The ERM frameworks draw on the principles of integrated risk management, in particular in that they seek to establish enterprise-wide 'risk registers' that capture a firm's net exposure to various risk factors.

But IRM efforts in practice are more than just these core principles. The reference to the board of directors points to a key feature of ERM, namely the involvement of senior managers and directors in a joint effort to achieve sound risk management. The emphasis here is on the *process* for risk management as much as the technical aspects of IRM. Roles and responsibilities are clarified and routines are set up so that no major risks are neglected. This aspect of ERM is sometimes referred to as 'risk governance'.

ERM also involves building up a 'risk culture'. While this is a somewhat nebulous term, it generally refers to the creation of a common terminology and frame of reference. A more unified approach is sought where things like units of measurement are standardized, which facilitates comparisons of different risky activities. The idea is that more consistency in decision-making is obtained by using similar definitions and methodologies across the company.

The ERM literature furthermore emphasizes success factors like having unwavering management support, and one or more 'ERM champions' that promote ERM internally. Often, a Chief Risk Officer is appointed, who oversees the ERM initiative and heads the risk committee, an interdisciplinary body of professionals that meet to discuss risk issues from the point of view of the whole firm. This would normally include specialists and senior decision-makers from the risk function, finance, strategy, tax, internal audit, as well as representatives of the business units.

We view the risk committee as a key success factor for a transition to a more integrated form of risk management. In the case of FXRM, the main implication is that FX policy would be an issue on the agenda of the risk committee rather than purely a matter for the treasury department. The risk committee, in this view, becomes a 'loop' in which to hammer out the optimal FX policy given the firm's strategic objectives and overall risk–return profile. Treasury, of course, would still have a key role in its capacity as specialist. Crucially, the FX policy would now be determined alongside the policies concerning other risk factors, such that they are set jointly based on a framework that balances pros and cons of different policy alternatives for the firm.

Key Chapter Takeaways

➤ Integrated risk management means viewing the risk–return profile as it relates to important corporate 'bottom lines' like cash flow, earnings, and financial ratios.
➤ Integrated risk management furthermore is based on the principles of viewing the exposure to each risk exposure on a net basis, and considering any diversification effects from risk factors being less than perfectly correlated.
➤ The opposite of integrated risk management is a 'silo-based' approach, in which each risk exposure is managed in isolation.
➤ FXRM has historically been a classical silo activity, defined and controlled by treasury.

➤ Firms are recommended to view FXRM as part of a board-supervised process of integrated risk management.

➤ In such an approach, FX policy would be proposed by a risk committee dedicated to managing the risk and return of the firm as a whole.

➤ Under such an approach, FX policy would effectively be determined alongside the policies concerning other risk factors. The goal is to balance the pros and cons of different policy alternatives for the firm in order to arrive at an optimal risk–return profile.

➤ Integrated risk management is greatly facilitated by developing an integrated decision support model.

Further Reading

Aabo, T., J. R. S. Fraser, and B. J. Simkins. 2005. The rise and evolution of the chief risk officer: Enterprise risk management at Hydro One. *Journal of Applied Corporate Finance* **17**, 62–75.

Andrén, N., H. Jankensgård, and L. Oxelheim. 2012. Exposure-based cash-flow-at-risk for value creating risk management under macroeconomic uncertainty. In Fabich, M., L. Firnkorn, U. Hommel, and E. Schellenberg (eds), *The Strategic CFO – Creating Value in a Dynamic Market Environment*. Springer-Verlag: Heidelberg.

Fraser, J. R. S., B. J. Simkins, and K. Narvaez. 2015. Enterprise risk management case studies: An introduction and overview. In Fraser, J. R. S., B. J. Simkins, and K. Narvaez (eds), *Implementing Enterprise Risk Management: Case Studies and Best Practices*. Wiley: Hoboken, NJ.

Chapter 9
Managing FX Risk Exposures

Many guidelines for risk management processes start with the recommendation to decide on the objective first. What is it that we want to achieve? Are we going to manage cash flow, net income, or something else? Unless the objective is stated in terms of managing a specific performance measure, the thinking seems to be that the process lacks purpose and direction.

We see it a bit differently. Corporate performance is too multi-faceted for that approach to work. More than one thing can be of high priority to the firm, and what is felt to be most important can change over time as circumstances change.

Our recommendation is instead to first of all get the basics right. A cost-efficient and well-functioning FXRM programme rests on certain pillars. When those are robustly in place, we can start thinking about how to actually manage FX exposures. A key aspect here is knowledge about exposures. FXRM, in our view, largely comes down to being good at monitoring FX exposures at multiple levels of performance. This should be the primary objective of the FXRM process.

At the end of the day, FXRM should be part of a broader framework for managing the firm's risk and return in a holistic manner. As discussed in the previous chapter, FXRM as a silo activity is getting increasingly difficult to defend. In a nutshell, exposures should be managed so as to keep the risk of breaching critical performance thresholds at acceptable levels, whilst maintaining an attractive upside potential for shareholders. Another hallmark of good FXRM is therefore the ability to understand how the risk of breaching key threshold levels of corporate performance is impacted by policy proposals related to FX exposures. In this chapter we discuss how to achieve this transition.

Getting the Basics Right

Throughout this book we have come across some fundamental principles and best practices of FXRM. Two important, and partly overlapping, pillars of FXRM are netting and centralization. They serve as a starting point in our discussion as they are about laying a sound foundation for FXRM, and they are briefly recapped here.

- **Manage aggregated net flows.** One of the most fundamental shifts in FXRM is to move away from hedging the exposures in each and every single commercial transaction. Some firms develop the habit of reflexively hedging any incoming or outgoing transaction, no matter how small. This leads to an overwhelming number of transactions that drive up costs. In any case, such hedging only achieves risk reduction in an exceedingly narrow sense. The firm really just eliminates the effect of FX variability on that specific receivable or payable during its brief life span – that is the whole achievement. Over time, consistent hedging of near-term transactions only results in the firm achieving the forward rate rather than the spot exchange rate. The forward rate is no less volatile than the spot rate, so the achievement is very modest indeed. Exposures instead need to be addressed on the level of aggregated commercial flows over a meaningful time horizon. The focus of attention is forecasted net flows (i.e. after considering natural hedges within the firm). These net flows relate in a meaningful way to variability in corporate performance (i.e. key bottom lines that management care about).

- **Manage exposures centrally.** Another fundamental transition in FXRM is to move away from a decentralized structure to a fully centralized approach. Fully centralized means first of all that headquarters exercise control over external as well as internal FX transactions. Centralizing transactions is associated with a number of well-known efficiencies, like achieving better rates and eliminating layers of administration. But full centralization also involves capping the business units' ability to set their own FX policy in terms of borrowing, depositing excess liquidity, and using derivatives. Centralizing the policy creates the necessary preconditions for a more integrated form of risk management in which FXRM ceases to operate as a silo. Business units, in contrast, are able to focus on what they do best, which is to optimize their business operations.

A Hierarchy of FX Risk Management Strategies

We now assume that the firm, through a coordinated effort between headquarters and business units, has been able to create a decent picture of its net commercial exposures, and that headquarters has a firm grip on FX transactions and policy. How can it actually go about managing its risk? There are three basic ways a firm can influence its exposure to foreign exchange rates. These are: natural hedges; derivatives (financial hedges); and the currency composition of assets and liabilities (primarily debt and the deposits of excess liquidity). While financial hedges often get most of the attention, to the point where some seem to equate them with FXRM, we instead argue that their use is limited to fine-tuning the risk profile in the short term. The liquidity of derivative markets thins out rapidly with longer maturities. When markets are not liquid, the bid–ask spread (an indicator of the cost of the hedge) increases. Even when longer-dated contracts are available, they tend to generate heavy effects on the financial statements due to fair value accounting. If a firm is forced to use its liquidity to cover margin calls on such fair value GLs, they can indeed turn into 'financial weapons of mass destruction'.

Natural hedges hold more promise in terms of reducing exposure to FX in a durable way. This strategy involves not just mapping out any existing offsetting exposures, but actively creating new ones. Firms can review their pricing and purchasing strategies and change them where possible so that the net exposure to any given currency is reduced. Imagine a firm that is currently selling the main part of its production in US dollars, while paying some input factors in euros. Perhaps the suppliers can agree to change their invoicing currency to dollars? Or perhaps some of the firm's customers are willing to pay in euros instead? Both these actions will reduce the net exposure to FX on an ongoing basis.

The idea is not to squeeze suppliers or customers into accepting a different pricing/invoicing currency against their wishes. They may be in a weaker position to bear such exposures, and resent having to deal with them. Such an approach may therefore be short-sighted and only lead to poorer relations with the firm's business partners. It is rarely worth it to lose business volume or reliable suppliers over FX issues. But there remain cases where changes that reduce exposure mismatches are possible without causing any upsets. Changing the currency of a business transaction may even fit better into the net exposure of the counterparty, and thus create value both for seller and buyer. Boosting natural hedges in this way can create more permanent reductions in exposure at little or no cost to anyone involved, in contrast to financial derivatives, which only have a risk-reducing effect until the maturity of the contract.

Importantly, an effort to create additional natural hedges needs to be orchestrated centrally. That is, it is not recommendable to start such a project before the firm has achieved a high level of centralization of FXRM. If business units go about making such modifications based on their own view of exposures, there is no guarantee that the overall outcome will be beneficial for the firm as a whole.

The guidelines from headquarters should also outline how units should evaluate whether the firm is still getting a fair deal when product prices are expressed in different currencies. Interest rate differentials affect the list price stated in different currencies, leaving some scope for misunderstandings and even mischief.

Firms can also use flexibility in production strategies as a means to lower the impact of adverse exchange rate movements. Flexibility is a very general risk management strategy. The easier and less costly it is to switch between different modes of operation as circumstances change, the less risk the firm has. Adapting easily to a changing world is a less risky position than being stuck or heavily invested in a particular way of doing things.

In an FX setting, flexibility could mean the ability to easily move a larger fraction of production to a foreign facility. If the firm has a long net exposure (i.e. more sales than costs) in a particular currency, it can, to the extent it has a manufacturing site there, seek to expand the share of its production that takes place in that country. This would normally lead to less production in another currency regime. If the firm was net short in that currency, it has achieved a more balanced net exposure in terms of both currencies. For this reduction in risk to be worthwhile, however, it must first be ensured that cost and quality are not negatively affected. If there are cost and/or quality issues from making such a move, it may turn out to be a very expensive form of risk management. There may also be so-called switching costs, which are costs related to the very act of implementing the change. However, any such flexibility that may exist should be part of a firm's review of its potential FX risk management strategies, and in favourable cases be seriously considered.

While flexibility is potentially risk-reducing, it is important to see that, if two production strategies are equal in terms of cost and quality, the firm should always locate production to the country which leads to the most favourable outcome in terms of FX net exposures. Then the firm obtains, on an ongoing basis, a lower net exposure to fluctuations in exchange rates. The issue of flexibility – and switching between different production strategies – is actually only relevant when one is willing, at times, to produce in a certain currency regime despite the fact that it leads to a larger net exposure going forward. If a firm mainly produces in Switzerland but exports to the USA, it may prefer to let its single US-based manufacturing site operate at full scale to lower its overall exposure to the dollar. But when the dollar is considered strong it can actually shift production to its sites in Switzerland to temporarily benefit from a *larger* net exposure, only to reverse the move when the dollar depreciates sufficiently.

It should be noted that shifting production in this way involves taking some kind of opportunistic view that the dollar is either over- or undervalued. Take, as an example, a situation in which the Swiss firm initially considers the cost of the two alternatives to be equivalent, in home-currency terms, after considering things like labour unit costs and expenses related to shipping, etc. It therefore prefers to run its US site at full capacity to reduce its net exposure to the USD/CHF exchange rate. Then the dollar appreciates by 15%. This is beneficial overall because it has a net long exposure due to its sales in the US markets. The appreciation also tempts the firm's manager to switch some of its production out of the USA and back to its Swiss sites. Because the dollar is now more 'expensive', the company can improve its operating margin by such a move. But it must involve a view that the USD/CHF is unlikely to go back to its initial level, because the shift means that the firm not only incurs the implementation costs but also foregoes the reduction in net exposure that comes from producing in the USA. Alternatively, if the managers initially assessed the alternatives to be equally attractive, but *believed* the dollar would strengthen, they might also have sacrificed the exposure reduction by choosing to produce in Switzerland. This is similar to how selective hedging works: the firm makes a judgement call that it perceives to increase the expected mean of performance, but that leads to more performance variability from not choosing the position that would minimize the net exposure to the exchange rate.

In certain cases, the firm can only enjoy the advantages of flexibility if it makes an upfront investment in it. Certain arrangements may have to be set up, and new logistics solutions found, for the alternative production strategy to be a viable option. But once in place, it will start to yield benefits in terms of allowing the firm to choose between two alternative modes of operation where current circumstances dictate the preferred option. This brings us to fairly advanced analytics, because calculating the value of optionality requires more complicated formulas than the standard net present value projection of cash flows. We do not discuss these option-based calculations further here, but believe that the general idea – investing in flexibility as a means of mitigating risk – should be explored in FX as in other areas of risk management. However, one should also be realistic about the implementation costs over and above the initial investment. Any switching between production sites may have serious consequences for personnel and other stakeholders involved, and damage future relations.

In certain cases, the acquisition of another firm leads to the creation of an alternative production strategy. Some academics indeed seem to view international acquisitions as a form of FX risk management, or 'operational hedging' as it is referred to. A new production unit can of course have a very large and possibly favourable impact on the firm's net exposures (this all depends on the circumstances, however – acquiring a foreign firm can also lead to more exposure to FX). We hesitate to think of acquisitions as an FX risk management tool in the proper sense of the term. Acquisitions should be primarily driven by an analysis of the size of the acquisition premium vs the value of the synergies that can be realized from the deal. The hefty premium usually involved (say 30% over the current market value of the target firm) cannot easily be justified using a reduction in FX risk as the main argument. If the deal leads to a more favourable situation in terms of FX exposures, then that would of course count as a positive in the overall scorecard. But then that is largely a positive by-product, which is a very different thing compared to pursuing international acquisitions using FX risk reduction as pretext.

Managing the currency composition on long-term liabilities (and certain assets) occupies a place in between natural hedges and derivatives when it comes to being effective at reducing risk on a sustainable basis. Borrowing in foreign currency means that the firm will pay interest (and eventually repay the loan) in that currency, which offsets any exposure the firm may have from its commercial activities. Let us say that a loan in a foreign currency is fixed rate over eight years. Then the firm has a known set of foreign-currency flows over this period that are not subject to renewal of contract terms.

A reasonable base approach to managing FX exposures, then, is to fully explore any natural hedges that are available, and then borrow with medium- to long-term maturities in foreign currency. FX derivatives are a potentially useful complement to this basic approach. They offer a flexible tool for adjusting exposures in the short to medium term. In the fast-changing economy of today, a need to change the risk management strategy can arise quickly and unexpectedly. This is where derivatives have a role to play.

Balancing Economics and Financial Management

The previous paragraphs did not discuss the accounting conse-quences of different FXRM strategies. In finance, the tendency is indeed to evaluate risk management decisions from an economic point of view, oblivious to any accounting issues. Unfortunately, things are not that simple in the real world. Companies struggle to manage and communicate several aspects of their performance, most of which are heavily influenced by accounting numbers. The attitude that 'it is just accounting' is therefore not realistic. One of the core messages of the book is that an effective FX risk manager needs to strike a balance by factoring in the potential for unrealized GLs (and margin calls) that come with different risk management strategies.

In this context it is useful to distinguish between three types of firms: the domestic exporter; the consolidated group with for-eign marketing units; and the consolidated group with foreign pro-duction units. The possible variations on these themes are almost endless, and they overlap in many respects. However, these stylized representations help clarify certain aspects of the trade-offs involved.

- **The domestic exporter.** This refers to a company with head-quarters and production in the home country that generates an FX exposure through exporting its goods to foreign markets. In this case, the main exposure is on commercial transactions, as there exists no foreign subsidiary exposed to translation risk. As noted above, foreign-denominated debt is a hedging strategy that matches commercial inflows with financial outflows (interest expenses and instalments) with a longer maturity than what is usually available on FX derivative contracts.[1] While bank loans tend to come with financial covenants, they are generally free of margin calls related to unrealized losses, which can be a great nuisance in terms of their impact on liquidity management. The immediate accounting consequence of borrowing in foreign currency is that the company will start to experience unrealized GLs in its net income, making it more volatile according to this performance metric. Now, this does not have to be a problem. Especially non-listed organizations may choose to view them as essentially 'paper volatility' and therefore a non-issue, in the secure knowledge that the basic risk management strategy is sound. If the firm instead uses derivatives, the same argument applies: the resulting fair value GLs can just be accepted. If the company *does* view these unrealized GLs as problematic, however, it may consider hedge accounting. Designating a foreign-currency loan as a net investment hedge, with the purpose of keeping the GLs of the loan out of net income, is not feasible in this case. The predicament of the domestic-exporter type of firm is that there is no subsidiary whose equity counts as the hedged item. For derivatives, verifiable transactions exist, making hedge accounting possible. But here is a genuine trade-off: while a derivative strategy allows the company to keep its net income free from unrealized GLs, it only does so at considerable administrative effort and expense. Not only does the firm have to go through the ordeal of applying

---

[1] Using the same logic, a firm that is net short a certain currency in terms of its commercial exposure will normally benefit from placing surplus cash in that currency. When the currency strengthens, the firm loses on its commercial side but gains on its financial assets.

hedge accounting to the derivatives, it also gives up the more durable risk reduction that comes from borrowing long term in foreign currency.

- **The consolidated group with foreign marketing units.** At some point a firm may take the step of acquiring a foreign subsidiary, or building up a presence in a foreign market through a newly created subsidiary. This is a game-changer so far as FXRM is concerned, because it introduces the translation exposure that comes with translating assets and liabilities in foreign subsidiaries. A company must understand and actively manage these translation effects because they are likely to influence important financial ratios. In one particular respect, the presence of a foreign subsidiary provides a small bonanza because its equity now constitutes the hedged item necessary to apply net investment hedge accounting. Net investment hedge accounting is a simple and straightforward process, at least compared to valuing and documenting the effectiveness of derivative contracts. It allows the firm to keep the unrealized GLs from its foreign-denominated loans out of net income with a more reasonable effort. In fact, borrowing in foreign currency makes even more sense now, because the need to translate the loans reduces the net AL position created by the foreign subsidiary. A foreign-currency loan, in comparison to a home-currency loan, therefore leads to less volatility not just from a cash flow perspective but also in terms of shareholders' equity for this type of organization. When the foreign subsidiaries are marketing units, without any production or independent purchasing of raw materials, exposure management can be centralized by the parent company. The parent company invoices the marketing units in their functional currency so that their payables are not exposed to exchange rates. To the extent that they sell exclusively in the local market, no mismatch occurs. Likewise, the financing of the units can be made in the units' functional currency through internal loans. This keeps the financial accounts of the marketing units free of exposures and FXRM firmly concentrated to headquarters.

- **The consolidated group with foreign production units.**
  Now we change the assumption regarding the foreign subsidiaries. They are no longer mere marketing units that bring
  the company's products to local markets. Instead, they are
  fully fledged operating units. This is another game changer in
  FXRM because it unleashes the full scale of complexity in terms
  of transaction and translation exposures. Because they are
  producing units, the subsidiaries will need to purchase input
  factors and sell their products to some degree independently
  of the parent company. It is very rare that this takes place
  without cross-border transactions going on. In fact, a producing
  subsidiary can – to all intents and purposes – be a multinational
  company in its own right! The complexity of the situation
  quickly escalates and becomes overwhelming when more
  than one subsidiary is involved. To prevent complete disarray,
  headquarters must strive to move from a transaction-oriented
  approach to managing anticipated net flows on a group basis.
  This transition is key. They must also pursue a high degree of
  centralization of FXRM. A decentralized approach is a recipe
  for a low degree of control. A firm may attempt to get a grip on
  aggregated net commercial exposures through a 'bottom-up'
  approach if it can ensure high-quality and consistent forecasts
  from its units. When this fails, as it frequently does, we have
  proposed using a statistical exposure model (the MUST analysis
  discussed in Chapter 2) to capture commercial exposure to
  FX. This allows the firm a cost-efficient way to cut through
  the complexity and establish an average relationship between
  an exchange rate and corporate performance. These exposure
  coefficients indicate by how much performance tends to change
  when an exchange rate changes, and therefore provide insights
  that help design borrowing and derivative strategies in ways
  that lower overall risk.

  As for translation risk, it is important not to lose sight of
  the fact that for calculating the net AL asset position in each
  currency it is the subsidiary level that counts. A firm may
  organize itself into business areas or divisions, and so on, with

their own set of financial statements, which introduces an intermediate translation stage. However, when these accounts are translated into the functional currency of the parent, all the effects of these cross-translations disappear. The same actually holds true for commercial cash flows. It does not matter if the subsidiaries' cash flow first has to be translated into the functional currency of some intermediate organizational unit, after which it is consolidated into the company accounts. However, if corporate performance is measured in the functional currency of the consolidated corporate group, which is strongly recommended, then one needs to consider mismatches between functional currency and transaction currency in order to create the exposure matrix. The objective with the matrix is still to understand variability in corporate performance as measured in the functional currency of the company. It is just that for this specific purpose we need to map out mismatches that create an indirect exposure to different cross-rates.

Due Diligence of FXRM Policy Proposals

The characteristics of an effective process for managing FX risk have been outlined in this chapter. Excel at understanding exposures to FX on multiple levels of performance. Shift away from a transaction-based approach to managing aggregated net cash flows. Centralize both FX transactions and policy. Under central purview, maximize the scope for natural hedges through a review of pricing and purchasing strategies. Create and utilize flexibility in production when economical to do so. Adapt the borrowing strategy to match financing flows with commercial exposures. Use derivatives on a limited basis as a way to flexibly adjust the risk–return profile in the short to medium term.

What is missing from this picture is a platform for making decisions related to FXRM on an ongoing basis. We opened the chapter by saying that it is futile to try to once and for all conclude which performance measure should be targeted in the overall risk management process of the company and therefore also FXRM. The multifaceted nature of corporate performance means that firms will care about more than one thing at any given time. The emphasis may furthermore change over time as circumstances change.

Some fairly robust insights can be teased out, however. Risk management theory most strongly supports the management of cash flow vs cash commitments as an objective of FXRM. As treasurers say, you can mess up anything but liquidity. Liquidity shortfalls can put the firm in serious trouble and impair its ability to compete and create value. This therefore provides a first benchmark for evaluating an FXRM proposal. Does the proposed FX policy meaningfully impact the risk that cash flows fall short of cash commitments, beyond what the company can deal with through its borrowing capacity? If the answer is yes, this would count as a strong pro in the assessment of the proposal.

There are also quite possibly real consequences from breaching critical threshold levels of performance in terms of financial ratios, such as triggering debt covenants. This provides a second benchmark for evaluating a proposal to manage FX risk. Does the proposal have a meaningful impact on our ability to meet these threshold levels of performance? Again, the pro-side of the proposal is credited if it can be demonstrated that it clearly does. Last in the hierarchy are earnings-based motivations for FXRM. Here it must be shown that convincing arguments exist in favour of using FXRM to prevent net income volatility. While fairly nebulous in our view, possible additions to the pro side are cases where the hedge makes it more likely to meet analysts' targets and there is a generally positive effect from being able to report stable earnings over time.

The point is that the pro side of the FXRM policy must be built up on an ongoing basis, especially when it comes to major proposed changes. How the pros stack up depends on the firm's current circumstances. Then, of course, the pros must be weighed against the costs of FXRM, which can be substantial. While glorified in textbooks, especially derivatives lead a problematic existence in organizations. They create a whole range of undesired consequences in practice: the need to be valued on an ongoing basis; volatility in net income from unrealized GLs; clutter in financial accounts; the cost from incurring a bid–ask spread; the cost from administrating the hedge; the tendency to multiply and be abused for reasons related to speculative behaviour and managerial compensation plans; and frequent surprises from being poorly understood. These are all good reasons to keep a tight lid on derivative usage in firms.

FXRM as Part of a Framework for IRM

The evaluation of the pros and cons of FXRM policy is greatly facilitated by an adequately equipped decision-support tool. Because of the complexity of FX exposures, a model is quite necessary for any effort to make informed decisions regarding FXRM. First of all, such a model would need to contain a description of the firm's commercial exposures to FX. But we also recommend that the accounting rules related to assets and liabilities in foreign currency are implemented, including the exposure matrix (as laid out in Chapters 3 and 4). Doing so leads to a dynamic model with enough accounting integrity to reliably guide decision-makers about the impact of FXRM on multiple levels of corporate performance.

Especially derivative strategies must be subjected to a proactive diligence. They have multiple effects on accounting numbers and liquidity that many people are not even aware of. An integrated tool of the kind we propose allows these consequences to be highlighted and understood before any decision is taken. It is important to examine scenarios in which the exchange rate strengthens or weakens substantially. Usually there is a focus on the risk-reducing effect in a 'down scenario' that comes from matching a derivative payoff with a commercial exposure. But the impact on net income, equity, and liquidity can be of concern even in an 'up scenario'. While the firm is benefitting from a stronger commercial performance, the unrealized loss on the derivative can have a detrimental effect on shareholders' equity or trigger margin calls that lead to highly unwelcome drains on liquidity. We are aware of several instances where precisely this has happened. Senior decision-makers must be made aware of these aspects before any decision is made, and sign off on the possible effects on performance from derivatives across a range of scenarios.

In our experience, integrated models of the kind envisioned here greatly increase the quality and quantity of the information available to support FXRM decisions. But they also tend to encourage a more integrated mindset and pave the way for a holistic view on the firm's performance. In that sense, the model actually 'leads the way' because it allows managers to see how everything is interconnected. Seeing how things hang together in a dynamic model promotes a different perspective on the management of the firm. It helps us break out of narrow silo mindsets and start taking a broader view on the firm's risk–return profile.

Integrated risk management thus happens much more easily with a model that addresses all the relevant exposures and performance measures in a single framework that combines cash flows, earnings, and balance-sheet effects. When also equipped with a user interface for evaluating different policy alternatives, it becomes a highly effective decision-support tool. One example of this is the financial planning and risk model of Hydro, mentioned in Chapter 8. Besides a rich description of exposures to FX and other risk factors, the model contains functionality for attaching different 'cases' to the existing profile. A case can be a proposal to increase the investment budget, acquire another firm, or hedge an FX exposure, to mention but a few possibilities. Several policy changes can also be evaluated together as a joint proposal. Such a model gives immediate feedback on how such cases affect the company's performance on multiple levels, and the risk that critical threshold levels of performance are not met. The firm's managers can then use this information to proactively evaluate whether the proposal is sound, given its contribution to both upside potential *and* downside risk (how this can look more specifically is covered in Chapter 10). Such a framework allows managers to design FXRM in such a way that it contributes to bringing risk to acceptable levels while maintaining an attractive upside potential. FXRM as part of a broader framework for managing the company's risk and return in an integrated way is then a fact.

Key Chapter Takeaways

➤ Corporate performance is too multifaceted to allow firms to decide once and for all the purpose of FXRM in terms of specific performance measures.

➤ A successful FXRM is characterized by a high degree of centralized control, and by moving away from a focus on near-term transaction exposures towards managing aggregated flows on a net basis.

➤ A company can modify its exposure to FX in a durable way by modifying its invoicing and purchasing processes to benefit from offsetting exposures where available.

➤ Changes in the currency composition of assets and liabilities, notably debt, allow firms to create positions that offset the commercial exposures on a medium- to long-term basis.

➤ Derivatives, in contrast, are mostly suitable for adjusting undesired near-term exposures.

➤ Theory is most supportive of using FXRM to manage the risk of cash flow falling short of important cash commitments, but consideration should be given to other potentially important performance measures, such as financial ratios.

➤ On a general level, any FXRM activity should aim to reduce the likelihood that performance falls below threshold levels that would trigger negative consequences.

➤ FXRM should be viewed as part of a broader effort to manage risk on a company-wide basis to find an attractive balance between risk and return at any given time.

➤ Such a company-wide effort is greatly facilitated by a decision-support tool that links FX exposures to performance measures and different policy alternatives.

Further Reading

Alviniussen, A. and H. Jankensgård. 2009. Enterprise risk budgeting – bringing risk management into the financial planning process. *Journal of Applied Finance* **19**, 178–192.

Jankensgård, H., A. Alviniussen, and L. Oxelheim. 2016. Why FX risk management is broken – and what boards need to know to fix it. *Journal of Applied Corporate Finance* **28**, 46–61.

Chapter 10
Communicating FXRM

E ven at this point, despite the amount of ground covered, we are not quite done yet. Even if the firm's capabilities in FXRM are sufficient to cover the areas described in the previous chapters, we must also find a way to communicate FX exposures effectively. This communication needs to take place on two fronts: internally, towards the company's decision-makers, and externally, towards the analysts and investors who take an interest in the firm's performance.

Communicating FXRM is important for several reasons. It is part of the organization's broader policy for disclosing information, which is what helps bridge the information asymmetry between the firm's management team and participants in the financial markets. At stake is nothing less than the company's transparency and general credibility, both of which are factors that determine its cost of capital. If the firm has put its FXRM house in good order, it has every reason to convey this to the outside world and gain further benefits from its efforts.

In the pages that follow, we argue that firms often get risk communication wrong in one of two ways: either by disclosing too little (not providing the relevant information) or by disclosing too much (cluttering the financial reports). In unfortunate cases, firms get it wrong on both accounts simultaneously.

What we advocate first and foremost is that the company's leadership start viewing risk communication, in general, as a strategic goal under their direct purview as an explicit part of the firm's FXRM programme. Since the firm's transparency is at stake, which in turn impacts its cost of capital, it is much too important to be delegated to the accounting or finance departments, or be decided by consultants in a local context.

Perspectives on Corporate Disclosure

According to some academic theories, there are benefits from disclosing more information and becoming more transparent. The background for this argument is that the participants in financial markets are at an information disadvantage compared to the firm's management team, who knows all the details about the company's expected performance, but selectively chooses what reaches outsiders. This unevenly distributed information is problematic. Among other things, it makes it harder to agree on financial contracts. Potential new investors have reasons to suspect that managers make decisions that primarily benefit themselves and/or existing shareholders, for example, by issuing shares when they think the company is overvalued.

The benefits of additional disclosure, in the traditional view, come in many guises. For example, the firm may experience an increased liquidity in the trading of its shares. This happens as more investors observe that there is an even playing field in terms of the information available about the organization, and therefore feel comfortable trading in its securities. Alternatively, the company enjoys a reduction in its cost of capital, either directly when issuing new securities, or indirectly in terms of having a lower discount rate applied to the valuation of its expected future cash flows. The latter point is the same thing as saying that its share price will increase. On an intuitive level, if the market trusts the firm's management team and gives it the benefit of the doubt, the firm's value tends to go up. Being perceived as good and reliable when it comes to disclosure of information is thought to boost this general trust.

But there can be too much of a good thing. A more recent perspective on disclosure is that many firms are in fact producing too much of it, at least in certain areas. The growth in the number of data points in annual reports has in fact been exponential over the last couple of decades. It turns out that investors may actually have difficulty making sense of all the detailed information and essentially fail to see the wood for the trees, a phenomenon known as 'information overload'. Excessive disclosure is sometimes also referred to as 'clutter', and has the paradoxical effect that the transparency actually decreases when there is more information.

The above suggests that it is important to strike a balance between providing enough value-relevant information to meet investors' demand and thereby earn their trust, on the one hand, and avoiding information overload, on the other hand. This balance has been referred to in the academic literature as 'optimal transparency'.

FXRM is part of this picture because the firm must decide how to present its risk management activities to the outside world. Disclosure about risk exposures, and related management activities, are key elements in a broader policy concerning investor communication. After all, assessing an organization is largely about trying to understand the potential risk and reward that comes from investing in it. A report by the CFA Institute from 2016 found that 90% of analysts find risk disclosures useful and use them in company evaluations, suggesting that they are indeed eager to understand firms' risk exposures.

FXRM Communication: Too Little or Too Much

Based on the preceding section, we have that firms are liable to underperform with regard to FXRM communication in one of two main ways: by disclosing too little, or by disclosing too much, thus failing to achieve optimal transparency. Both carry their own set of problems and lead to a higher than necessary cost of capital.

The problem of too little FXRM disclosure is partly driven by the current accounting standards. The reporting requirements, as per IFRS or US GAAP, are quite peculiar in that companies are really only supposed to disclose guidance concerning the risks related to their portfolio of financial instruments. IFRS 7, for example, calls on firms to report on the nature and significance of risks related to financial instruments. Risks are divided into three categories: credit, liquidity, and market. For each of these, qualitative and quantitative guidance is expected.

The one-sided focus on the financial instruments themselves is another glaring inconsistency affecting FXRM created by the standard-setters. What ends up happening is that these instruments are taken wholly out of the context of the business transactions they supposedly hedge. Information about financial instruments is of quite limited usefulness when there is no corresponding information regarding commercial exposures. The main task of FXRM is not to manage the risks that arise from a portfolio of financial instruments: it is about determining which portfolio of financial instruments makes most sense given the firm's commercial exposures!

The CFA Institute report finds a presently low level of content among analysts with firms' risk communication. One source of frustration is the lack of meaningful quantitative disclosures. Another is that organizations do not reliably supply investors with explanations regarding the principles, or reasons, behind their FXRM decisions. When such information is lacking, a firm's FXRM activities are hard to understand. The CFA report concludes that 'risk disclosures are difficult to understand because of their incomplete nature and often-fragmentary presentation', going on to say that 'qualitative disclosures are uninformative and are often not aligned with quantitative disclosures' and that 'top-down, integrated messaging on overall risk management is missing'.

The previous paragraphs suggest a problem of too little information: meaningful sensitivities of commercial performance and a narrative about FXRM are often lacking. However, FXRM also plays a part in the information overload problem, primarily because financial instruments are subject to onerous disclosure require- ments. Many firms engage in detailed and complex disclosures about their financial instruments, thereby adding to clutter in financial reports. This is especially true if hedge accounting is applied. As discussed in Chapter 6, the highly specialized rules and terminology surrounding this topic make reading financial statements sometimes a struggle. The volume of text necessary to check the disclosure box on hedge accounting appears to be considerable.

Another potential problem related to excessively detailed information about derivatives is that, though intended to reassure investors about management's oversight and control, it may in fact make the company seem riskier. That is, simply drawing investors' attention to the scope of derivative usage may trigger concerns about what these positions might entail. Remember that derivatives have been implicated in a large number of highly publicized scandals that have brought misfortune on the firms using them. Investor sentiment towards derivative disclosure may therefore, unless management has earned their trust, be fundamentally negative.

It is quite possible to suffer from problems of too much and too little FXRM disclosure at the same time. There may be excessive reporting of financial instruments and related hedge accounting, while the firm simultaneously fails to produce a decent commu- nication of commercial exposures and a narrative to connect the commercial exposures and its FXRM activities.

Exposures vs Sensitivities

What, then, given these concerns, is a sensible approach to FXRM communication that comes reasonably close to achieving optimal transparency? We posit that the typical analyst or investor is interested in four sets of facts. The first is a quantitative estimate of the sensitivity of the firm's commercial performance to changes in exchange rates. The second is the corresponding estimate of the sensitivity of the company's portfolio of financial instruments (mainly derivatives and debt). The third is the net of these two estimates, which is the firm's net sensitivity to changes in exchange rates. Using this number, the analyst can calculate the net impact on performance under different FX scenarios. The fourth is some kind of qualitative description of the company's overall risk management approach (i.e. the thinking and philosophy that guides its risk mitigation actions). Not being able to understand or anticipate the actual net exposures, or how the firm might act in the future, adds to the impression of a black box. FXRM therefore needs to achieve a modicum of predictability, which is achieved by the narrative aspects of disclosure.

Sensitivities have a central role in any effort to communicate FXRM. This book has, so far, mostly framed the discussion in terms of corporate *exposures* to foreign exchange risk. Exposures and sensitivities, while closely connected, are not the same thing. This begs the questions of how they relate to each other and how to transit from one level to the other.

Let us begin by recapping what exposures are. They can be thought of as economic magnitudes given by the firm's business activities (or balance sheet items). Based on our discussions in Chapter 2, we know that conceptually a company's operating cash flow is given by the equation $Q * P * XR$, where Q is quantity, P is price, and XR is the exchange rate. In this equation, exposure to any one of the three variables is given by the product of the other two. Exposure to the exchange rate, therefore, is given by $Q * P$. This produces the amount of foreign currency that needs to be converted into home currency. For example, for a Norwegian oil producer the number of barrels extracted times the average sales price (in US dollars) in a specific time period constitutes the exposure to the USD/NOK exchange rate.

A sensitivity is a way to normalize an exposure by defining the size of the percentage change in the underlying market risk factor. For example, a one-unit change in the price of oil does not have the same meaning as a one-unit change in an exchange rate because the scales are different. This is why we must normalize it by selecting a percentage change which can then be applied uniformly across different types of market risks.[1] For example, sensitivities may be defined as the change in performance to a 1%, 5%, or 10% change in the exchange rate.

Let us illustrate this idea behind a sensitivity. Assume that the numbers for Q and P are 15,000 and 500, respectively, for a German exporter of electronics, where P is a price quoted in US dollars. USD/EUR is given as 0.80. The expected cash flow in euro terms is therefore $15,000 * 500 * 0.8 = €6,000,000$. The exposure to the exchange rate, in contrast, is $15,000 * 500 = US\$7,500,000$. To get the sensitivity to a 1% change, we first have to compute this number. In this case, it would be given by $1\% * 0.8 = 0.008$, rendering a new exchange rate of 0.808. A 10% change would be given by $10\% * 0.8 = 0.08$, rendering an exchange rate of 0.88. The next step is simply to apply the chosen change to the exposure. The 10% sensitivity would be given by $US\$7,500,000 * 0.08 = €600,000$. This is the sensitivity of the German firm's performance to a 10% change in the USD/EUR exchange rate.

Observe that a sensitivity is the difference in performance, as measured in home currency, from applying two different assumptions for the exchange rate to the exposure: $(0.88 - 0.8) * 7,500,000$. To generalize, the sensitivity is the exposure multiplied by the chosen percentage change in the exchange rate.

An analysis of the exchange rate in unit terms would not work. A one-unit change in the USD/EUR would mean that the exchange rate goes from 0.8 to 1.8. Not only is this clearly unrealistic, it also puts different currencies on an unequal footing. Had the firm been a Swedish exporter instead, and the original exchange rate 8,

---

[1] The comparison is not completely fair even when exposures are normalized as a sensitivity, however. This is because the market risk factors have different levels of volatility. The oil price, for example, is more volatile than the average exchange rate (i.e. it fluctuates more over time). This means that a 10% movement in the oil price over the specified time horizon is *more likely to happen* than for an exchange rate. This probabilistic dimension is a relevant input in an analysis of risk. But we do not pursue this advanced form of risk reporting further here, based on the argument that this is information available to the analyst and something he or she can factor in on their own when constructing different scenarios.

a one-unit change would imply a new rate of 9. While still a substantial change, it is clearly less unrealistic than a one-unit change for the USD/EUR. In percentage terms, the change is a lot less in the case of the Swedish krona. This is why the analysis should be done by consistently applying a percentage change *of the same size* to all exchange rates to which the firm is exposed.

Constructing Sensitivities

The first step in constructing useful sensitivities, then, is to decide on which percentage change is going to be applied. Which order of magnitude is chosen is not of great consequence, as long as the firm is consistent in applying it to all exchange rates. However, sensitivities to a 10% change in the exchange rate seem to be the norm, and come recommended in this book as well. It is a change that is economically meaningful whilst at the same time being something that could realistically happen.

The second step involves deciding for what level of performance we are going to express sensitivities. One of the major themes in this book has been that corporate performance is multifaceted and that firms should be deft at quantifying exposures at many levels. This is always a core skill, but when communicating we do not enjoy the luxury of having a great deal of time and space to cover all the nuances of various performance measures. Risk communication must be effective and simple.

So, given this, what should we choose out of all the possible dimensions of corporate performance? A sensible place to start is probably EBIT (income before interest and taxes). This is a measure that targets operating performance that most corporates and analysts use regularly in their assessment of firms. It is quite possible to adjust it in various ways to get an even cleaner measure of 'core operating performance', but for effective communication it is probably best to refer to the numbers as given by GAAP (i.e. EBIT as reported in the firm's financial reports). Making too many adjustments, despite good intentions, quickly leads to a situation where it becomes hard to understand what we are actually talking about if different companies are all using their own definitions.

Reporting EBIT sensitivities may in some cases be enough. It captures first and foremost commercial exposure, which is what analysts are most concerned about. A possible complementary piece of information could be net income sensitivities. These sensitivities take taxes and net financial expenses into account. Particularly the latter is potentially important to consider, because it is where many of the strategies to manage FX risk have a financial impact. That is, the gains and losses related to FX derivatives and loans in foreign currency would normally appear on that line. Therefore, the net income sensitivity, if reported alongside the EBIT sensitivity, gives an idea about the extent to which the firm's FXRM policy balances out its commercial exposures.

Step three in constructing a sensitivity involves selecting the time frame. Here, there are really only two options: a quarterly or a yearly basis. Most often, absent heavy seasonality in performance, it would be inconsequential which is chosen as one is easily re-expressed in terms of the other. A reasonable base approach would be to report sensitivities in terms of yearly performance numbers but, if seasonality is an important matter, provide additional information regarding any quarterly patterns.

One must also decide on whether sensitivities are to be reported individually (per exchange rate) or as a sensitivity to a simultaneous weakening (or strengthening) of the home currency vs all foreign currencies. Some companies prefer to express their exposures as a 'grand total' impact that would occur under the assumption that the home currency moves by the same percentage against all currencies to which the firm is exposed. To some extent they have a case, as we could see in Chapter 8, in that there is a home-currency effect creating a positive correlation between most exchange rates for any given home currency. However, combining the sensitivities in such a way reduces the overall information content, and it will be harder for the analyst reading the report to build their own scenarios of performance using different sets of assumptions for specific exchange rates. Therefore, it is better to show sensitivities for each exchange rate to which the firm has a major exposure. The sensitivity to a broad weakening (or strengthening) of the home currency may be added as a complement.

To summarize this section so far, a good starting point for communicating FXRM is to report the sensitivity of yearly EBIT and net income to a 10% change in the top one to five exchange rates to which the firm has commercial exposure.

A possible extension is to provide sensitivities for alternative measures of performance that are of relevance to the firm in question. It could be the case, for example, that the firm has large exposures to translation risk. It might therefore be of interest to analysts to understand how changes in exchange rates play out in terms of certain financial ratios. Again, such effects are best communicated through sensitivities because that allows for meaningful comparisons between different exchange rates. For example, that could read as: 'On average, due to translation effects, company ABC's debt-to-equity ratio increases by 12% for every 10% increase in the USD/SEK exchange rate, and 7% for every 10% decrease in the EUR/SEK exchange rate.' While analysts may gratefully receive such information, it should be remembered that it is well beyond what the reporting standards call for. It is up to each firm to decide whether providing this service is worthwhile.

Generating High-Quality Sensitivities

The sensitivity of performance to changes in exchange rates may be clear enough at the conceptual level. In practice, we run into the complication that many firms struggle to generate high-quality estimates of their exposures (recall our discussions in Chapter 2). Obviously, any sensitivity provided will be on a best-effort basis and suitable disclaimers may be added to clarify this aspect of sensitivities published in financial reports.

The sensitivities provided to guide investors can, as an alternative to the heavy and error-prone bottom-up process, be obtained by applying the MUST methodology. In fact, regression analysis of past performance is often a very reasonable and cost-effective approach to generate sensitivities. Sensitivities obtained in this way can be put to another use, which takes communication of FXRM to another level. By filtering out the effects of exchange rates on past performance, one gets an estimate of the firm's *sustainable* performance. Sustainable performance should here be understood as performance unaffected by the 'headwind' or 'tailwind' created by exchange rates in any given period. A Swedish exporter, for example, might be experiencing a windfall from a stronger US dollar, but at the same time be on a negative trend in terms of cost efficiency. The currency windfall would temporarily hide this decrease in sustainable performance from the analyst's view.

To illustrate the idea of filtering out FX-induced noise from performance, consider a Swiss firm exporting to the German market. It has established an EBIT sensitivity to a 10% change in the EUR/CHF exchange rate of 7%. In one quarter its EBIT increases by 6% and the Swiss franc strengthens by 11%. Is this increase in EBIT good or bad? While 6% is seemingly a decent number, it is in fact entirely driven by the FX tailwind. According to its sensitivity coefficient, the FX-induced windfall is $7\% * 1.1 = 7.7\%$. This is by how much EBIT, on average, would increase simply due to a change in the exchange rate of that size. Since the actual increase in EBIT was only 6%, its sustainable performance is in fact developing negatively by $6\% - 7.7\% = -1.7\%$. Rather than celebrating the boost in reported EBIT, the firm's managers and directors should be worrying about its poor sustainable performance and search for measures that improve it.

Many of the company's stakeholders have an inherent interest in sustainable performance. Making such numbers available would therefore increase transparency and establish a firm as top-notch in terms of disclosure. Managers tend to be disinclined towards communicating underlying performance, however, because there is a favourable asymmetry in that they can claim credit for good performance (boosted by currency windfalls) but blame exchange rates when they move against the firm.

As regards the sensitivity of net financial expenses to changes in exchange rates, things look a bit different with respect to how they should be quantified. Here, a regression analysis approach is less promising because of the often high rate of change in the portfolio of financial instruments. In general, a bottom-up technique is the preferred alternative as it allows a more precise quantification. This means generating the sensitivity of financial expenses through a modelling of the actual positions in foreign currency loans and FX derivatives. It is about specifying, in a spreadsheet application, the link between these loans and derivatives, on the one hand, and the firm's performance, on the other hand (as captured by net financial expenses). The modelling of these positions should reflect the principles outlined in Chapters 3, 4, and 6, so as to describe as correctly as possible not only the realized payoffs but also the full set of consequences for performance from translation effects.

We are aware that this is a tall order for many firms. There is a possibly very large number of contracts involved and keeping track of all of them analytically may be beyond the capabilities of most organizations. The ledgers that register financial transactions generally do not communicate with the spreadsheet applications that managers use to analyse and predict performance. But some version of the 80–20 rule applies. A firm can concentrate on the most important positions that have a meaningful impact on performance.

Preferably, the bottom-up modelling of financial positions should take place within the context of the kind of integrated decision-support tool that we discussed in Chapters 8 and 9. In our experience, a unified analytical spreadsheet application is a very powerful support in terms of evaluating not only FXRM, but basically any kind of major corporate policy. Assessing FX derivative positions and FX loans only makes sense when viewed in the context of the firm's overall performance. This task is greatly facilitated by a decision-support tool that links *both* commercial performance and financial positions to key bottom lines like EBIT and net income.

Sensitivities: Putting It All Together

Equipped with a spreadsheet application that contains a description of both commercial cash flow and financial positions, the rest is quite easy. Just have the model deliver its estimates of performance under two sets of assumptions, and take as sensitivity the difference between the two estimates that result. The first set of assumptions should be the expected exchange rates, which is to say the firm's best estimate of future rates. These are the forecasts managers actually believe in. The second set of assumptions should be the ones that reflect a 10% change compared to the best estimates.

The results from this exercise can be compiled in a table such as Table 10.1. For the selected exchange rates, the firm reports the impact on EBIT, net financial expenses, and the final effect on net income (income after tax).

Such a table nicely connects commercial performance and the effects from FXRM (as they manifest themselves in net financial expenses). Therefore, it gives investors and analysts a better chance to explore the firm's risk and return profile by applying their own sets of assumptions.

One possible objection is that the sensitivity of financial expenses captures 'noise' such as translation and revaluation effects, which distort the comparison between the operating and financial levels of performance. What the ambitious firm can do is decompose the effect on financial expenses into two parts: one for realized (cash-effective) payoffs, the other for valuation and translation effects.

Table 10.1 Sensitivities

	IMPACT (MN/SEK)		
	EBIT	Net financial expenses	Income after tax
SEK/USD 8 ⇒ 8.8	467	220	193
SEK/EUR 9 ⇒ 9.9	110	62	39

Managers may, in the absence of a quantitative breakdown of realized vs unrealized effects, discuss the extent to which unrealized effects generally tend to impact the reported numbers. This part of the financial report is an excellent opportunity to clarify some of these principles. It is where the firm can explain where these unrealized effects come from and the logic behind having in place positions that generate such effects. This kind of communication should serve to reduce any potential negative investor sentiment that such noise might create (and therefore also lessen the need for hedge accounting).

Moreover, the discussion in this section of the report should also cover the firm's general philosophy regarding FXRM. In many respects, one of the main weaknesses of today's practice in risk communication is the lack of a broader narrative. Organizations may well comply with disclosure requirements and check all the relevant boxes. But they remain notoriously weak when it comes to providing the kind of narrative that would connect the dots and make FXRM understandable to outsiders. Now, this may be for a reason: managers may not actually have much in the way of a systematic approach, and rather enjoy the freedom it implies to take speculative positions. We have argued in this book that such discretion should be minimized to achieve a certain level of predictability. But to the extent that a firm's FXRM rests on certain foundations, these should be communicated in order to increase transparency. A narrative could be centred around the issues of how the main commercial exposures arise; in what ways the derivative and loan positions are thought to offset these exposures; under what circumstances the firm normally hedges; the objectives thought to be achieved by hedging; how these positions ultimately impact performance; which organizational unit(s) are doing the hedging; and so on.

As for the mandatory disclosure related to financial instruments, managers must choose between three forms of disclosure. The first is the tabular form, in which details like nominal amounts, maturities, and forward rates are shown. The other two are a sensitivity or value-at-risk figure. The value-at-risk figure is a summary statistic that describes how much a portfolio of financial instruments stands to lose with a given probability. For example, a firm may state that due to market risk, its derivative portfolio is expected to lose no more than US$5 mn with a 95% statistical confidence. This is equivalent to saying that its managers are 95% certain that the loss on the portfolio will not exceed US$5 mn.

We recommend that firms comply with these requirements by using the tabular form of disclosure. A value-at-risk figure is too opaque, relying as it does on a large number of assumptions. It is almost completely devoid of any meaning anyway. Because it ignores the commercial side of things, it is detached from the broader context of the firm's overall risk–return profile. A table, however, describes the actual portfolio in a transparent and intuitive way. It shows the derivatives in place on this particular balance sheet date, which gives important clues as to the extent and type of hedging instruments the firm is inclined to use. Any speculative positions involving, for example, exotic derivatives would then be on display, reducing the potential for unpleasant surprises.

Internal Communication of FXRM

So far, we have largely focused on how to communicate FXRM to external stakeholders like investors and analysts. We now turn our attention to internal communication. What do we mean by this? The first point is that corporate policies are decided by the firm's management team and board of directors. To make informed decisions they rely on internal resources, such as the accounting, tax, and strategy departments, to prepare the necessary material (sometimes aided by consultants). In the case of FXRM, the decisions to be made revolve around whether or not to take certain actions to mitigate FX risk. The second point is that the relevant support for these decisions would normally come from the finance department, or a risk function (here we include the risk committee that we discussed in Chapter 8). These are the functions that have the required expertise, and quantitative tools, to address these issues in a qualified way. Internal risk communication refers to how they can illustrate the consequences on risk and return from the various decision alternatives that the firm's leadership are evaluating.

One can be forgiven for thinking that the constraints in terms of time and space are now lifted. In some respects, this is true. A firm can devote significant resources to analysing FXRM. However, it can definitely still be a challenge. Anyone who has stood in front of a board of directors or senior management team to check FXRM off the agenda in 15 minutes or less will appreciate this point. The directors are highly busy people, and FXRM is but one point of the agenda.

What should the staff responsible for the analysis of FXRM communicate in this brief window of time to the firm's own senior decision-makers? The table of sensitivities is a good starting point for internal communication as well. Presumably, the company's top management are also interested in the firm's main exposures and what is being done to balance them out through active FXRM. The information put forth in Table 10.1 does a good job of informing about these core issues.

One major difference is that internal communication also needs to address the issue of *what these exposures mean for the firm's ability to meet its performance thresholds*. Some kind of action would be prompted by an assessment that the current configuration of net exposures implies an unacceptably high risk that these thresholds are breached. Recall that FXRM in this book is viewed as managing the variability of corporate performance with respect to exchange rates. More specifically, it is about managing the risk that performance falls below crucial threshold levels, the breaching of which could be argued to trigger negative consequences.

It is substantially more challenging to communicate how FX exposures impact the prospects for meeting performance thresholds. Sensitivities do not involve a probabilistic dimension. They merely indicate how exchange rates and performance relate to each other under two different sets of assumptions. Understanding the prospects for breaching threshold levels, however, does require some assessment of how likely that is to happen, or how far removed the firm is from such an outcome. It matters for decision-making whether the company is near a critical threshold or whether it is at a safe distance from it.

To make FXRM communication more relevant for decision-makers, we recommend implementing a *distance-to-threshold analysis* (DTA). A DTA has two components. The first is showing the firm's expected performance under current policies and assumptions about exchange rates. The second is the company's performance if policies and/or exchange rates were to change. If it is considered that the firm would end up too close to a threshold, managers can act on that information and proactively change the FXRM policy.

The general idea is that changes in exchange rates *and* changes in policy combine to move the organization either closer to or further away from its threshold level of performance. Internal communication is about creating an understanding among key decision-makers regarding the joint impact of these two drivers of risk. There are always alternative courses of action; policies that could be implemented in place of the current ones. At any given time, swapping part of the loan portfolio into foreign currency, or selling more currency forward, are possibilities. What the most suitable configuration of FXRM policies is can change over time, so it makes sense to continually revisit these alternative policies and get attention on whether some action should be taken. The existing policies should not be taken for granted. They may have been put in place without much conscious thought regarding the firm's overall risk–return policy, and should therefore be critically assessed on a *pro et contra* basis.

The DTA analysis makes FXRM more interesting to decision-makers because it highlights how their own decisions drive the firm's risk profile. This is in contrast to the standard exercise of going through the three different 'good–expected–bad' scenarios, which leaves them largely passive. The DTA addresses the following dimension: 'if we do this (i.e. change a policy), what are the consequences for the risk (and return) of the company?' The explicit link between the actual decisions made and what happens with the risk profile helps to generate good discussions about what is the best way forward with respect to FXRM.

Table 10.2 illustrates a DTA. The setting involves a Swedish exporter with a major exposure to the US dollar. The performance metric chosen is cash flow-to-cash commitments (CC), which is operating cash flow net of the sum of various cash commitments like capital expenditure, dividend payments, interest expenses, and loan instalments. A negative CC means that the firm is unable to meet its cash commitments through internally generated cash flow, and instead must rely on its cash balance or external financing to uphold them.

In the base case in Table 10.2 the expected exchange rate is 8.0 (this is the firm's forecast of the exchange rate). Two scenarios for the exchange rate are then investigated: a 10% weakening of the Swedish krona against the US dollar (which produces a new exchange rate of 8.8) and a 10% strengthening (USD/SEK = 7.2). Likewise, two policy changes are investigated: a discontinuation of the current hedging programme and a decision to swap the firm's entire debt into US dollars. The critical threshold level of performance is set to zero. Perhaps the company only has a modest amount of cash to support its cash commitments in the event that the CC turns negative. Or perhaps it has a weak balance sheet and therefore limited abilities to attract new external financing. Such factors could make the firm's managers disinclined to see the CC go to zero, which therefore makes for a suitable reference point in its risk analysis.

Table 10.2   Distance-to-threshold analysis

| | Cash flow-to-cash commitments (mn/SEK) Threshold: CC = 0 | | |
	Strategy 1: Leave as is	Strategy II: Discontinue hedging	Strategy III: Swap debt into USD
USD/SEK = 7.2	CC = 96	CC = (112)	CC = 225
USD/SEK = 8	CC = 390	CC = 390	CC = 390
USD/SEK = 8.8	CC = 640	CC = 812	CC = 512

Based on Table 10.2, the firm's decision-makers would be able to see that a discontinuation of the hedging programme would imply a breach of the target were the dollar to weaken to 7.2. This may be an unacceptably short distance to that threshold, in which case they would decide against it despite the fact that the upside potential is now somewhat higher (812 vs 640 mn/SEK). The strategy of swapping debt into dollars reduces risk even further, while necessarily also capping more upside potential. If the managers feel that the distance to the threshold is too close for comfort also in the base case scenario (96 mn/SEK), they might decide swapping is the preferable strategy. If the USD/SEK ends up strengthening to more than 7.2, the firm is in danger of a breach of the threshold even under the as-is strategy.

The distance-to-threshold analysis is a powerful tool for figuring out the firm's so-called 'risk appetite'. This term refers to the search for the appropriate amount of risk to take in the pursuit of upside potential. It is hard to arrive at a well-informed idea about risk appetite without some reference to the critical threshold level of performance and an assessment of how likely that is to occur. The DTA illustrates the company's risk profile as a function of not only external risk factors, but also the firm's own decision-making. Furthermore, the DTA highlights how the organization's upside potential is affected by the same policies. The DTA, by visually presenting the distance to key performance thresholds as well as the associated upside, combines the risk and return dimensions and therefore constitutes a good basis for determining the value-maximizing decision.

This book has stressed the need for a good understanding of exposures to FX for various measures of performance. Internal communication is about making sure that there is a link between the quantitative information about exposures and the decision-making process. Any benefit from taking a decision to mitigate an exposure to FX, we have argued, comes from reducing costs that are associated with falling below critical threshold levels of performance. Whether those performance thresholds are defined in terms of cash flow, net income, or financial ratios is firm-specific, or even situation-specific. To appreciate the impact from risk mitigation strategies, specific decision-support tools should be developed that connect exposures to FX and performance (and by extension the threshold levels of performance). As illustrated in the DTA analysis, the ability to run various scenarios for exchange rates, while at the same time evaluating policy options discussed by management, is an especially powerful combination.

Another point that we have emphasized in the book is that any FXRM decision must be accompanied by a realistic assessment of the drawbacks of risk mitigation actions. We have pointed to several such potential disadvantages: in particular, they may cap upside potential; create volatility from fair value changes; introduce the risk of margin calls that disrupt liquidity planning; and reduce transparency in financial reports. An advanced decision-support tool that incorporates the principles outlined in this book will have some of these features built into it, allowing for immediate quantitative feedback. Even lacking such a tool, firms should strive to think through and where possible quantify the magnitude of the potential drawbacks. By paying attention to the multiple consequences of risk management strategies, management ensure that they are not caught by surprise, and that a value-creating trade-off between the pros and cons of different strategies can be made.

Key Chapter Takeaways

> Risk disclosure is important to bridge the information asymmetry between a firm and participants in the financial markets. How it is done influences the firm's transparency and therefore its cost of capital.
> According to current reporting requirements, it is only mandatory to disclose information about risks related to the firm's portfolio of financial instruments, leaving the more important commercial exposures as a voluntary disclosure.
> Sensitivities are exposures multiplied by a specific percentage change in the exchange rate in question.

➤ A good starting point for communicating FXRM is reporting the sensitivity of yearly income before interest and taxes (EBIT) to a 10% change in the main exchange rates the firm is exposed to.

➤ The EBIT sensitivities can be complemented with the corresponding 10% sensitivity of net financial expenses, which is where the payoff from FX derivatives and FX loans tends to end up.

➤ A narrative that outlines the firm's general approach to FXRM is important to help investors and analysts understand the quantitative disclosures.

➤ For internal communication, the sensitivities should be complemented with an analysis of how alternative FXRM policies impact the risk of breaching important performance thresholds.

➤ A distance-to-target analysis maps out how FXRM policies and sensitivities combine to produce a certain risk–return profile for the firm as a whole, allowing for a more proactive approach to FXRM.

Further Reading

CFA Institute. 2016. User perspective on financial instrument risk disclosures under international financial reporting standards. Downloadable at https://www.cfainstitute.org/en/advocacy/policy-positions/user-perspective-on-financial-instrument-risk-disclosures

Oxelheim, L. 2003. Macroeconomic variables and corporate performance. *Financial Analyst Journal* **59**, 36–50.

Oxelheim, L. 2019. Optimal vs satisfactory transparency: The impact of global macroeconomic fluctuations on corporate competitiveness. *International Business Review* **28**, 190–206.

Index

Note: Page references in *italics* refer to figures and tables.

199